# *ABC*

# *of*

# *Reading*

# *TRG*

Talonbooks • Vancouver • 1999

TALONBOOKS
104 — 3100 Production Way
Burnaby, British Columbia V5A 4R4, Canada

The publisher gratefully **Canadä**
acknowledges the financial
support of the Canada Council for the Arts; the

THE CANADA COUNCIL | LE CONSEIL DES ARTS
FOR THE ARTS | DU CANADA
SINCE 1957 | DEPUIS 1957

Government of Canada through the Book
Publishing Industry Development Program;
and the Province of British Columbia through the British Columbia
Arts Council for its publishing activities.

Printed and bound in Canada by Hignell Printing Limited

Talonbooks are distributed in Canada by General Distribution Services,
325 Humber College Blvd, Toronto, ON, Canada, M9W 7C3; Tel.:
(416) 213-1919; Fax: (419) 213-1917.

Talonbooks are distributed in the U.S. by General Distribution Services
Inc., 4500 Witmer Industrial Estates, Niagara Falls, NY 14305-1386
USA; Tel.: 1-800-805-1083; Fax: 1-800-481-6207.

CANADIAN CATALOGUING IN PUBLICATION DATA
Jaeger, Peter, 1960- ABC of Reading TRG
(The New Canadian criticism series)
Includes bibliographical references and index.
ISBN 0-88922-423-4
1. McCaffery, Steve – Criticism and interpretation.
2. Nichol, B.P., 1944-1988 – Criticism and interpretation.
3. Toronto Research Group – History and criticism.
I. Davey, Frank, 1940- II. Title. III. Series.
PS8575C33Z75 1999    C811'.5409
C99-910808-5    PR9199.3M29Z75 1999

# Acknowledgements

Frank Davey deserves immense thanks for sharing insights on both the published and unpublished history of the TRG, and for his enthusiastic support of this project from its earliest stages as a Ph.D. dissertation at the University of Western Ontario. I'm especially grateful to Tilottama Rajan for her detailed responses to the book's theoretical components, and to Charles Bernstein, Manina Jones, Patrick Deane, and Anthony Purdy for their thoughtful and challenging comments during my defence. The thesis stage was funded by a highly appreciated Social Sciences and Humanities Research Council of Canada doctoral fellowship.

Thanks are due as well to the two anonymous Humanities and Social Sciences Federation of Canada readers whose comments helped shape this book's final form, to the Federation for the subvention which supports this publication, to Steve McCaffery for generously answering questions about the Group, to my friends and colleagues Keith Haartman, Margaret Toye, Scott Pound, Karen Mac Cormack, Bill Howe, Jeff Derksen, Kim Simon, Jenifer Papararo, Tom Orange, Darren Wershler-Henry and Christian Bök for encouragement along the way, and to Redell Olsen for proof-reading help. Thanks also to my family for catching my drift.

I wish also to thank Ellie Nichol and Steve McCaffery for the following permissions: "Man in Lakeland" and the excerpt from *ABC The Aleph Beth Book,* both by bpNichol, reproduced with the permission of Ellie Nichol, the two pages from *Carnival: the first panel,* reproduced with the permission of Steve McCaffery, ad the panels from "Narry-a-Tiff," reproduced with the permission of Steve McCaffery and Ellie Nichol.

Finally, I wish to acknowledge that this book has been published with the help of a grant from the Humanities and Social Sciences Federation of Canada, using funds provided by the Social Sciences and Humanities Research Council of Canada.

for my son Julian

# Contents

*Plot is product within linguistic wrapping. Dictionaries and directories work against this status by throwing emphasis on to the single page and the information stored thereon.*
—The Toronto Research Group


*Capitalism begins when you open the dictionary.*
—Steve McCaffery

# Operating Instructions

*ABC of Reading TRG* is not about what the Toronto Research Group's reports are about, but about what they invite us to think about. Steve McCaffery and bpNichol formed the TRG in 1973 as a forum to investigate issues pertinent to formally imaginative writing, such as the role of the reader, the material status of the book, and the non-semantic aspects of translation and narrative. The earliest TRG reports build on theories proposed by such writers as Gertrude Stein, Jerome Rothenberg, Ilse and Pierre Garnier, and the Brazilian *Noigandres* group of concrete poets. After 1974, however, the Group integrates ideas drawn from French poststructuralist theory into their research reports; McCaffery claims that he and Nichol had read Edmond Jabès, Jacques Derrida, Roland Barthes, and Jacques Lacan by this time (*Rational* 17). This book responds to the TRG's engagement with theory by constructing a relationship among theoretically inflected readings. On one hand, it reads their reports "against the grain"—i.e., it attempts to uncover the unconscious links among repressed affective and political elements that circulate throughout their writing. This approach predominantly entails situating them in the shadow of perspectives developed by Lacan, Fredric Jameson, and Slavoj Žižek. On the other hand, it also reads the TRG sympathetically by underlining their construction of a positive, productive desire which does not centre on lack, but which actively celebrates multiplicity and affirmation, an approach that chiefly entails reading them in the light of theories proposed by Barthes, Gilles Deleuze and Felix Guattari, and Julia Kristeva. *ABC of Reading TRG* juxtaposes these seemingly antagonistic and incommensurable critical operations, in order to delegitimate the illusion that they are complete and self-sufficient. If this method raises more questions than it answers, it is consistent with McCaffery's and Nichol's frequent calls for a productive reader who does not, in McCaffery's words, assume a "prescriptive and appropriative stance before its object field" (*Rational* 13). This book answers the hail of the TRG, while simultaneously subjecting that hail to critical scrutiny.

McCaffery and Nichol often seemed unproblematically to accept the authority of the theorists whose works were most influential during the period of their collaborations. Their tendency to support an all-encompassing social and aesthetic revolt is as much indebted to the political background that informed European theory during the late 1960s as it is to the apocalyptic breaks with the past that were current among the baby-boomer counter culture in North America during the same period. Perhaps in the less idealistic terms of the present moment, the Group's revolutionary agenda could be historicized as the construction of a salvational story—a desire for Utopia—rather than as the outline of a viable critical theory. In effect, theory functioned for the TRG as a site for the organization of desire; 'theory' in their texts could be read as an ideologically-charged object which organizes desire, not only for the Group itself, but also for their readers. The act of theorizing is a cultural practice that structures the enjoyment of a particular social cluster, and the TRG's assimilation of theory into poetics therefore orders a very specific (albeit limited and critical) form of social cohesion. Despite this un-selfreflexive element in the TRG's reports, their work remains critical because of its refusal to organize desire around such typical Canlit tropes as the authentic voice, the land, or Canadian identity. From the start, the Group engaged in dialogue with a transnational context of aesthetic, philosophical, and ideological issues.

Along with their consideration of European theory, McCaffery and Nichol were also highly influenced by the 20th-century tradition of disjunctive literary Modernism. Peter Quartermain describes this tradition as a writing that is "recalcitrant to description, ambiguous, highly wrought, apparently disjointed and even vacant (which is to say, seemingly 'about' nothing at all)" (3). In the North American context, a skeletal genealogy of disjunctive poetics could be drawn through the work of Stein (whose writing Nichol introduced McCaffery to early in their friendship), Louis Zukofsky, John Cage, the Black Mountain poets and the Language writers[1] (among many others). McCaffery's work is for

---

[1] The terms "Language writing," "Language-centred writing," and "Language poetry" broadly refer to a group of texts by writers who share an "interest in the question of reference, a question which they see as having its social and political as well as aesthetic consequences" (*North* 110). More specifically, the terms refer to a collection of texts by writers including McCaffery, Charles Bernstein, Bruce Andrews, Lyn Hejinian, Barrett Watten, and other writers published in the journal

Quartermain exemplary of disjunctive poetics because its elements undermine "ordinary decoding procedures," thus forcing readers to take account of both "individual particulars (each separate word) and the totality in which those words appear (the whole text)" (17). Similarly, Marjorie Perloff characterizes contemporary radical poetics as an art of "making strange" through indeterminate phrasal and sentence structure, a practice that "comes to us from Gertrude Stein, for whom image was never the central concern" (*Radical* 78-79). For both Perloff and Quartermain, "radical" or "disjunctive" poetics question reference and the materiality of the signifier, and the TRG's interrogation of conventional semantics place them within this tradition.

The TRG reports offer a useful springboard from which to examine McCaffery's and Nichol's individually-authored work. Readers of their "borderblur" writing will be aware of the difficulties inherent in generically distinguishing between their theoretical and aesthetic texts, and the development of one mode tends to influence the development of the other. The two writers shared many concerns, yet the differences between their writing are significant and should not be overlooked: McCaffery's Marxist agenda and polemical argument against the referent as a "commodity fetish" contrasts the residue of humanistic ideologies clustered around Nichol's problematic inscription of revealed versus non-referential meaning. Nichol's "use" of theory is implicitly humanistic; as Stephen Scobie points out, Nichol is prepared to use the vocabulary and ideas of poststructuralism, although he subsumes the anti-humanistic tendencies of contemporary theory into a desire to "clarify the soul & heart and deepen the ability to love" within a sympathetic community (*bpnichol* 17). While Nichol considers theory as a potential means to liberate the creative individual within a community of other like-minded individuals,

---

*L=A=N=G=U=A=G=E* (1978-82) and elsewhere. As Douglas Messerli points out, however, there is no "single definition or a unified complex of ideas which applies to 'Language' poetry" aside from the foregrounding of language itself, not as something that explains or translates experience, but as the source of experience itself (1, 2). While these writers employ a number of different strategies and approaches that are irreducible to a single stylistic form, Messerli considers Language writing as a "political action in which the reader is not merely required to read or listen *to* the poem but is asked to participate *with* the poet/poem in bringing meaning to the community at large" (3). See Bob Perelman's "Language Writing and Literary History" (1995) for a detailed discussion of this term.

McCaffery regards it as a means to investigate the production/expenditure of meaning in the reader/writer/text relationship, and to re-politicize the word within the broader social context of inter-subjective relations. He writes: "we must avoid a humanization of the reader who is not to be anthropologized as a 'person' but seen structurally as a theoretical location in a textual activity. This functional definition of the reader applies to *all* types of writing" (*North* 27). Nevertheless, both writers express a concern for the interpretive process in regard to a community of readers, and their texts thus invite discussion on the complex connections among reading, the desire (or lack of desire) for meaning, and social relations.

The title of this book deserves some explanation. *ABC* stems in part from Nichol's love of the alphabet, from McCaffery's concern for the materiality of the signifier, and from an ironic reference to the title of Ezra Pound's 1934 *ABC of Reading*. Pound's book is "not addressed to those who have arrived at full knowledge of the subject without knowing the facts" (9). *ABC of Reading TRG* addresses those subjects who have not arrived at full knowledge of the facts, because of the critical assumption that facts are only interpretations. It is structured in alphabetically ordered chapters, each of which is based on a text and/or theoretical concern discussed by McCaffery and Nichol. The alphabetical approach provides a non-chronological structure in which themes, forms, concepts, and images from earlier texts can be juxtaposed against later developments—a type of continuous genealogical present, a means to identify and question the persistence of returning conscious and unconscious elements, as well as their complete reversal, transformation, or absence. The book can be operated either conventionally by reading it from beginning to end, or it can be read by following chains of thought, indicated by superscript letters which link non-sequential chapters together—a device borrowed from *Book 5* of *The Martyrology*.[N] The rhetorical artifice of the alphabetical framework affords a means to preserve one of the TRG's most significant contributions to research writing on contemporary poetics, i.e., their simultaneous stress on both form and critical investigation.

# Alphabet

Nichol always wanted readers who would "seek to reach themselves and the other through the poem by as many exits and entrances as possible" (*Journeying* n.p). If we were to enter Nichol's various repetitions of the letter through the conjectural doorway of Lacanian psychoanalysis, we might find a means to critically re-consider the TRG's early citation of Pierre Garnier, who claims that "each letter inscribes its sound on the page ... and the music organizes itself in the unconscious. The page finally sings" (qtd. in *Rational* 53). As the discourse of the Other, the unconscious is always already a type of alphabet, a symbolic chain or series of metonymic displacements and metaphorical condensations. For this reason, the TRG's emphasis on the music of non-semantic letters does not necessarily remove the letter from meaning, but returns the letter instead to the messages of the unconscious. To paraphrase Lacan: determining the scope of what the letter repeats prepares the question of what the symptoms repeat.

Writing on the alphabet in "The "Pata of Letter Feet, or, The English Written Character as a Medium for Poetry" (1985), Nichol distinguishes between "normal" representation and his own creative procedure. Saussure's distinction between signifier and signified provides him with a theory of conventional representation: "i write the word 'dog' and i anticipate that you will, to some degree, envisage a dog" (81). He proposes an alternative to Saussure's theory, however, by writing alphabet texts which dispense with the signifier/signified binary pair: "when i write a letter i am not naming in the same way. i am creating a brand new 'A' or 'B'... the letter does not stand for something else in the way that, once again, the word 'tree,' say, stands for a tree" (81). Much like the letter in Lacan's "Seminar on 'The Purloined Letter'" (1956; trans. 1972), the "content" of Nichol's letters are never revealed. Both texts present the signified as insignificant; in Lacan's text the content of the letter is irrelevant compared to its capacity to constitute intersubjective relations among characters, while in Nichol's text the signified is immaterial to the visual surface of the signifier. To read the letter as non-representational is to illustrate its role as *objet petit a*—the object small other, which Lacan claims: "serves as a symbol of the lack, that is to say, of the phallus, not as such, but in so far as it is lacking" (*Four* 103). Unlike the big O Other, which refers to the differential structure of language and social relations that produce the subject, the small o other is a dream of fulfilment, an empty surface for the projection of desire. Nichol's alphabets dispense with a signified in order to foreground the signifier as full presence, yet the letters are not empty in the sense that they do not signify at all: they signify vacancy, the concept of absence. The letters thus function as *objet a*, fantasy substitutes for the missing phallus of full and complete presence. In effect, Nichol's alphabets are symptomatic of affect, of lack.

One of Nichol's early alphabets, titled *ABC The Aleph Beth Book*, provides a good example of his attempt to write outside of the signifier/signified opposition. The text consists of 26 letter overlays, bracketed at front and back by the same statement on poetics. Fragments from this statement are also reproduced around the edges of each letter. For Brian Henderson, the text's superimposition of individual letters resembles "a kind of mandala .... [used] for concentrating cosmic and psychic energy" ("New" 15). Henderson reads the letter S, for instance (fig. 1), as an analog to Buddhist images which attempt to empty the mind on its way to the void ("New" 17-18). Henderson concludes: "The simplicity of much of this work is a kind of serenity .... outside of time—an instantaneous lightening that empties the word, deprives it of being, at least as we know it, and makes space for a new existence" ("New" 26). By reading each individual letter as an instantaneous and single unit or as a mandala existing "outside of time," Henderson neglects to account for the sequential character of the alphabet. In Lacanian terms, the A to Z sequence of Nichol's text presents exactly the opposite of serenity and full presence, because it functions as a metonymic chain, a game of displacements which is not instantaneous but diachronic: "desire *is* a metonymy, however funny people may find the idea" (*Ecrits* 175). The alphabetic series thus situates the reader in the path of the symbolic. Reading the modified alphabet as emptiness is a mis-recognition which occurs through the repression of sequence and context: B precedes C and follows A, thereby forming an ordered symbolic chain. So the space for Henderson's alphabet as "new existence" remains a reworking of space occupied by the old existence, the symbolic order.

Scobie's claim that *ABC The Aleph Beth Book* evokes a "religious awe of the alphabet as origin" (*bpNichol* 47), exemplifies how a reader might affectively respond to the desire for origin evoked by the *objet a*. The

THE NECESSITY TO BE.

Fig. 1. bpNichol. "S." 1971. *ABC The Aleph Beth Book.*

word "awe" means among other things solemn and reverential wonder, tinged with latent fear, a cause of dread. When used to describe Nichol's text, these definitions illustrate the capacity of the alphabet to disturb the subject. The OED also associates awe with restraint, as in "to keep him in awe." If Nichol's alphabet keeps its readers in awe, it acts as a symbol of their lack, while simultaneously stimulating their desire. Readers of *ABC The Aleph Beth Book* are offered a text on which they might, in Lacan's words, "model their very being on the moment of the signifying chain which traverses them" ("Purloined" 60).[G]

Nichol's gloss on *ABC The Aleph Beth Book*, printed at both the front and at the back of the text as well as in segmented parts on each page, further illustrates how the text reiterates the constraints of the symbolic: "... WHAT HAS BEEN CONSTANT TILL NOW HAVE BEEN THE ARTIFICIAL BOUNDARIES WE HAVE PLACED ON THE POEM. WE HAVE PLACED THE POEM BEYOND OURSELVES BY PUTTING ARTIFICIAL BOUNDARIES BETWEEN OURSELVES & THE POEM. WE MUST PUT THE POEM IN OUR LIVES... "(n.p.). Yet the poem as alphabet is always already "in our lives," for the symbolic order which constitutes subjectivity exists through the differential structure of language: the alphabet signifies textuality. By expressing the typical contemporary trope of a blurring between art and life, Nichol's text underlines the dialectical work of symbolic textuality on the self, i.e. the self desires identity and presence (the imaginary), but is instead implicated in difference, absence, text (the symbolic). Therefore, even the imaginary "realphabet" developed by Nichol in "Re-discovery of the 22 letter alphabet: An Archaeological Report" (1981) and *art facts: a book of contexts* (1990) remains tied to the symbolic; both the real alphabet and the realphabet are textual, and in the Lacanian scheme, textuality is the precondition for lack. Moreover, Nichol's modification of individual letters in *ABC The Aleph Beth Book* and elsewhere does not necessarily mean that they escape the constraints of the symbolic; even if the alteration of an individual letter is intended to block or cancel the action of reference—i.e. if the letter does not assume the symbolic agreement—the existence of the letter as an element in a linguistic chain situates it in a symbolic constraint foreign to that intention.[B]

# Book-Machine

By Machine we mean the book's capacity and method for storing information by arresting, in the relatively immutable form of the printed word, the flow of speech conveying that information. The book's mechanism is activated when the reader picks it up, opens the covers and starts reading (*Rational* 60).

McCaffery's *Carnival The First Panel: 1967-70* (1973) is a mechanical device, complete with its own instruction manual. Readers are asked to destroy the book by tearing out its pages "carefully along the perforation" near its spine, and then to assemble the "panel" by laying out the pages in a square of four. *Carnival* offers its readers a productive role not only because they are asked to manipulate the book physically, but also because the text's instructions do not indicate the precise manner in which the panels are to be re-assembled. There are sixteen pages of "typestract" or abstract typewriter art in *The First Panel* (not including the covers, introduction, errata sheet, and postcard with instructions for reading); however, the order of combining the "sixteen square feet of concrete" panels is left up to the reader/operator of the text. As the TRG point out, *Carnival* is an anti-book: "perforated pages must be physically released, torn from sequence and viewed simultaneously in the larger composite whole. The work demands that language be engaged non-sequentially rather than in sequence" (*Rational* 65).

However, the TRG's erection of a binary between non-sequentiality and sequentiality is problematic, for as we have seen in the case of Nichol's *ABC The Aleph Beth Book*, this opposition assumes that the signifier is autonomous, and does not function as part of the signifying chain. Since *Carnival* is text, it remains a part of the conventions of textuality. Moreover, a reader's personal configuration of the panels merely substitutes another sequence for the author's absent sequence; in both cases language precedes the subject. In *Problems in General Linguistics* (1966), Emile Benveniste argues that pronouns are "constitutive of all the coordinates that define the subject" in the "instance of discourse" (227). For Benveniste the subject finds its identity within discourse through identification with the pronoun 'I' and in opposition to the pronoun 'you,' even though these terms may be reversed when uttered by another. The TRG's replacement of the writer by the reader follows a similar path, because both terms remain a part of the cultural coordinates that define subjectivity.

*Carnival*'s instruction sheet claims that the first panel is "sixteen square feet of concrete," but this claim is false advertising. Each of the sixteen pages actually measures only eleven inches by eight and a half inches, the actual contents of the package are less than the number advertised on the label. The theme of deception is further played out in the text's errata sheet (fig. 2), where one non-semantic signifier is exchanged for another. But because both of these signifiers have no conventional signified, the deception occurs by feigning deception, by pretending that there is a truth behind the error. McCaffery's errata sheet operates like one of the various forms of the joke told by Lacan to illustrate the paradoxical relationship between truth and deception in the symbolic. In the 1964 version of the joke, one character tells another he is catching a train for Lemberg: "*Why are you telling me you are going to Lemberg, the other replies, since you really are going there, and that, if you are telling me this, it is so that I shall think you are going to Cracow?*" (*Four* 139). In the 1957 version, however, Lemberg is labelled Cracow, while Cracow is labelled Luov (*Ecrits* 173). The shifting city names emphasize the point of this short narrative—that meaning lies not in a single signified but in intersubjective difference. Only one of the characters in the joke knows his destination, but in his attempt to communicate through language, his knowledge is perceived by the other as deception. McCaffery's substitution of one non-semantic destination for another similarly presents us with the paradoxical proposition "I am lying." Since neither of the sets of signifiers on the errata sheet are attached to a signified, the truth of the error is that there is a deception, which in turn is a truth. The only "truth" claim of this text is an ironic Nietzschean foregrounding of art as the site of true lies: "art treats *illusion as illusion*; therefore it does not wish to deceive; it *is true*" ("On Truth" 96). If we get the joke we become conscious that the Other evokes our unconscious desire through its capacity to defer a destination as full and present meaning. The joke lets us in on a piece of the real, because it

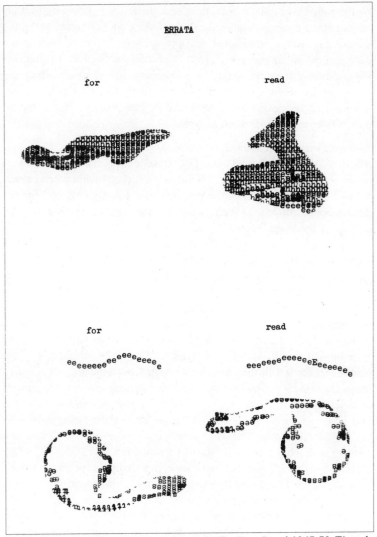

Fig. 2. Steve McCaffery. "Errata." *Carnival: The First Panel 1967-70.* Tipped-in postcard.

reveals how the anchoring points of truth and error are mythical con structs. Because both truth and error are presented as autonomous to the signified, they question the imaginary relationship attached to the signifier by the subject. In other words, the two signifiers are shown by McCaffery's joke to be images taken for the real. As Kaja Silverman notes, the signified is always provisional, and can never be "resolved back into a pure indication of the real" (165). *Carnival*'s refusal to resolve the signified into the real makes it a machine for short-circuiting the imaginary/symbolic complex. Like the unfinalizable destination of the letter in Lacan's story, McCaffery's joke illustrates that the Other has no punch-line, no terminal point of arrival.

*2. Once I was my Mommy then I Gave Birth to Letters*
*Absolute Statement for my Mother* (1979) is one of several book-machines customized by Nichol. The text is roughly 2 inches square when closed. When the machine is opened, it folds out into a single strip of 7 hinged panels, approximately 14 inches long. A single word is printed in black capital letters on each panel: "I / AM / I / MA / I / AM / I / MA ..." This machine operates as a psychoanalytic assembly line for the subject of language, for the inverted duplication of the AM MA pair recalls Lacan's narrative of subject formation. At the pre-Oedipal mirror stage, an infant who is sunk in its motor incapacity and nursling dependence, on seeing its own reflection in a mirror, will identify with its own specular image, and become the division between the I who watches and the I who is being watched. Because of this division the infant's "jubilant assumption" of a unified bodily image is imaginary. This split foreshadows in a primordial form a further breach that occurs once the subject acquires language, for by mistaking itself and its utterance as one, the subject assumes that it is the author of meaning—it misrecognizes itself as a unified being. Lacan's infant at the mirror stage attains imaginary self-consciousness through the act of seeing itself as an other reflected in a mirror. In Nichol's text, the mirrored repetition of "AM / I / MA" announces a desire for the full presence of pre-Oedipal experience, yet the representation of the pair in language points to the absence of the maternal signified. Language pulls the imaginary identity between AM, MA and I into the world of symbolic difference, away from the mother and into the Other. The text unconsciously holds up the misrecognition of a speaking self as "I," the unitary source of its own language, because in the sequence "MA / I / AM" the word "I" is split between on the one hand a speaking subject (the referent) and on the other hand the subject of speech (the referee). Any recognition of unity between the two "I"s is a misrecognition, because the subject is unable to designate fully its own presence as whole. Just as the subject at the mirror stage misrecognizes

itself as one with its own specular image, the subject in the symbolic fails to recognize the split between itself and its own utterance. So the *Absolute Statement for my Mother* is a statement of absolute desire for presence, which is forever frustrated but continually repeated.

According to the TRG, readers of book-machines are no longer simply consumers of texts, but instead "must adopt the role of operators, workers and machine hands" (*Rational* 182-183). By inviting readers to produce their own meaning, McCaffery and Nichol offer a political critique of the author/reader relationship, which is analogous to the producer/consumer relationship in capitalism. In "Deux pièces difficiles pour une même main" (1979), Caroline Bayard writes: "Le seul niveau de subversion pour le TRG est dans le corps linguistique: l'écrivain n'est ni prophète, ni révolutionnaire" (165). For Bayard, the TRG's supposed lack of a political agenda is at odds with Quebecois writers who published in *La Barre du Jour* during the same period:

Alors que les Canadiens sont fascinés par la restructuration de la page-surface au hasard, la destruction de la linéarité et le volume, la taille, l'esthétique des signes, les Québécois, eux, consacrent leurs énergies à la relation texte-réalité politique, texte-responsabilité politique" (169).

True, the TRG uphold the type of formal experiments cited by Bayard, but they also construct these experiments in the shadow of an ideological critique: in "The Search for Non-Narrative Prose," they write: "what is needed is not more fluid forms (because such an attitude hands control over to the forms themselves) but rather a more fluid writer/reader relationship: one in which, to use Barthes' phrase, the reader is 'no longer a consumer but a producer of the text'" (*Rational* 135). Later statements by the TRG, such as their 1981 discussion of the book-machine, bring politics more firmly to the foreground: "The book's primary status is that of object: a homogeneous mass-produced item subject to the forces of market economy, the general logic of commodities and the ideological effects of the cultural industry" (*Rational* 179-80). Contrary to Bayard's suggestion that the TRG's attention to form is primarily apolitical, the book-machine is consistent with Charles Bernstein's suggestion that stylistic innovation is recognizable not only as an alternative to aesthetic convention, but also as an alternative type of social formation (*Poetics* 227).

*3. The Book-Machine as Rhizome*

What would happen if we were to re-interpret the TRG's book-machine according to Gilles Deleuze and Felix Guattari's writing on productive desiring-machines? Psychoanalysis is for Deleuze and Guattari repressive to the extent that it binds the subject to a pre-ordained social order. Opposed to the (negative) Lacanian dialectic of lack and desire, they propose instead a theory of "desiring-production," which they define as a "pure multiplicity, that is to say, an affirmation that is irreducible to any sort of unity" (*Anti* 46). Desiring-production's multiplicities differ from Lacan's unifying and totalizing theory of the subject as lack; for Deleuze and Guattari, desire is a positive and pluralistic force that conditions the relations between humans, industry, and nature. "Everything is a machine," they write,

There is no such thing as either man or nature now, only a process that produces the one within the other and couples the machines together. Producing-machines, desiring-machines everywhere, schizophrenic machines, all of species life: the self and the non-self, outside and inside, no longer have any meaning whatsoever (2).

The TRG's claim that readers of book-machines "must adopt the role of operators, workers, and machine hands" (*Rational* 182-83) suggests that readers take on the role of productive desiring-machines that are intimately linked with other machines in an unceasing continuum: "one machine is always coupled with another" (5). Secondly, the body-machine and book-machine connection throws suspicion onto the structuralist notion that the author/reader relationship is analogous to the producer/consumer relationship. Instead of postulating a flow and flux of consumptions, productions, distributions, and points of reference, structuralism subjugates the multiplicity of desiring-production to a binary opposition between antithetical terms. The structure (reader : consumer : lack :: writer : producer : fulfilment) merely reproduces the historical condition of capitalist economics in another form. Reading the book-machine's operator as a desiring-machine in connection with a potentially infinite series of other desiring-machines, on the other hand, deterritorial-izes the binary structure's social coding and re-situates it as a type of schizophrenic anti-logic. Schizophrenia's disruption of the social norm cannot be totalized within a metaphysical system/symptom that is based on absence. For Deleuze and Guattari, the schizophrenic experiences the world as a process of production rather than as a dialectic of lack:

*production of productions*, of actions and of passions; *productions of recording processes*, of distributions and of co-ordinates that serve as points of reference; *productions of consumptions*, of sensual pleasures, of anxieties, and of pain. Everything is production (4).

The schizophrenic route of the desiring-machine invites a reconsidera-
tion of Nichol's non-referential letters as signifiers for the vacancy which

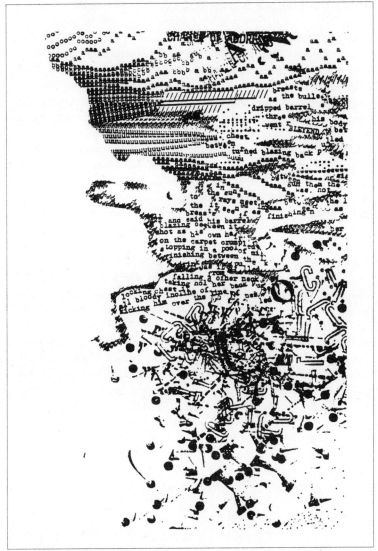

Fig. 3. Steve McCaffery. From *Carnival: The Second Panel: 1970-75.*

constitutes the subject as lack. The sequential character of the alphabet signifies deferral along the signifying chain rather than the full presence of an object, and Nichol's concrete alphabets feed their reader's desire for an impossible presence. However, if we re-consider Nichol's alphabet as a desiring-machine, that is connected to other desiring-machines, we deterritorialize the notion that lack forms the centre of subjectivity, thereby reterritorializing subjectivity as a rhizomatic network of multiplic-ities. Deleuze and Guattari describe how a "rhizomatic book" differs from a "root-book": the latter imitates the world through reflection (the "One that becomes two" [*Thousand* 5]), while the former occurs through "Principles of connection and heterogeneity: any point of a rhizome can be connected to anything other, and must be" (6). McCaffery's *Carnival The Second Panel* (1977; fig. 3) is similarly rhizomatic, since it assembles heterogenous typographies, colours, and rubber stamp marks, which can be dis-assembled and re-assembled by a desiring-machine who is already part of a multiplicity. Panel 2 intersperses the expressionist free play of non-semantic typography and rubber stamps among fragmented lines of linguistic text (eg. "psychologically / complex pressure / towards an inattention"), thereby setting up a dialogic relationship between picture and language. In 1987 McCaffery noted that *Carnival* is "a dialogic text and the presence of Bakhtin as a kind of unconscious presence in the composition of the panel is a thought with which I've often toyed" ("Annotated" 72). This dialogic relationship is similar to the Bakhtinian carnivalesque, because it constructs "on that space where the destroyed picture of the world had been—a new picture" (177). Panel 2 thus seems to exhibit the rhizomatic features found by Deleuze and Guattari in an assemblage: "The book as assemblage with the outside, against the book as image of the world" (23). However, as Christian Bök and Darren Wershler-Henry point out, the text's tipped in postcard bears an image of the entire panel in its assembled state, thereby reterritorializing the reader's role by offering a supplement that negates "the need to destroy the object through reading it" (n.p.). *Carnival*'s second panel invites readers to chart their own territory, while simultaneously providing them with a legend to map the tract.

# Canadada Concrete

## 1. McCaffery L'etranger

In 1970 at the book launch of *The Cosmic Chef*,[2] I was poked in the stomach by an umbrella. The assailant was Dorothy Livesay who had been told of my birthplace and who accused me—as a landed immigrant—of stealing publication space from more deserving (because "Canadian") writers (*Rational* 18).

McCaffery's anecdote illustrates the nationalistic climate in which the TRG began their research. Livesay's performative critique of McCaffery is paradoxical, however, since *The Cosmic Chef* is clearly indebted to the European and South American traditions of concrete writing. In the text's "afterward," Nichol writes: "this whole book is best described by the term dom sylvester houedard coined BORDERBLUR" (n.p.); the importation of a generic term by a non-Canadian writer in a Canadian anthology exemplifies the international context of this stream of poetic endeavour. The "Dorothy Livesay" that McCaffery caricatures legitimates the international movement, as long as it is practised only by Canadians in Canada.

This paradox might be analyzed with reference to Slavoj Žižek's remarks on ethnicity and the new political situations in Eastern Europe. Žižek reads the struggle between ethnic groups not only as a clash between different symbolic organizations, but also between different relationships toward enjoyment. This type of enjoyment is not the same as pleasure, because it denotes the "paradoxical satisfaction procured by a painful encounter with a Thing that perturbs the equilibrium of the 'pleasure principle'" (*Tarrying* 280). Enjoyment does not stem from unpleasure avoided, but from the subject's relationship towards its own

---

[2]Nichol edited *The Cosmic Chef Glee & Perloo Memorial Society Under the Direction of Captain Poetry Presents an Evening of Concrete Courtesy Oberon Cement Works* (1970), an anthology of concrete texts by 32 writers, including McCaffery, Michael Ondaatje, Margaret Avison, David UU, and Greg Curnoe.

objectified lack or void in the form of the "Thing"—i.e., towards an object that materializes the nothingness experienced by the desiring subject. For Žižek, nations function as sublimated materializations of the Thing. Nations are structured through the organization of enjoyment (as a response to lack) in cultural practices such as feasts, rituals of mating, and initiation ceremonies. Enjoyment is the non-discursive element that "appears" to subjects through these practices: a nation "*exists* only as long as its specific *enjoyment* continues to be materialized in a set of social practices and transmitted through national myths that structure these practices" (*Tarrying* 202).

In the Canadian context, the violence of Livesay's umbrella jab at McCaffery enacts the clash between on the one hand the newly emerging enjoyment of post-centennial Canada, and on the other hand, anxiety about losing national enjoyment to the older Colonialist order. If, as Žižek argues, the Nationalist Thing is a materialized form of the nothingness at the centre of the subject, McCaffery's presence at the reading threatened one of the most significant fantasies that structured Canada during this period; since for Žižek enjoyment is always a response to absence, Livesay's projection of anxiety epitomized Canadian lack in the late 60s and early 70s. McCaffery writes, "it was a milieu obsessed with establishing a Canadian identity largely predicated upon nationalist narratives and values" (*Rational* 18). In effect, that nationalist narrative derived its enjoyment from excluding the foreign Other.

*2. Denkgegenstandenkspiel*

In the introduction to the *Ganglia Press Index* (1972), Nichol writes that he discovered the term "concrete" in 1964. Although he had already been writing visual poetry in relative isolation from the international move-ment, he "didn't know the term concrete ... the word helped put a name to what at that point dave [aylward] & i were already into" (qtd. in Scobie *bpNichol* 32). In 1967 Nichol changed the title of *Ganglia* to *GrOnk*, in order to reflect his greater awareness of the international context of concrete, and the publication put Canadian writers in touch with experi-mental writing from Europe, Latin America, and Japan (Bayard *New* 107). Gomringer's 1954 theorization of *Denkgegenstandenkspiel* ("play activity"), in which the poet determines the "play-area," while the reader "grasps the idea of play, and joins in" (67), provides a good example of how this international movement offered a theoretical background for Nichol's and McCaffery's early concrete writing. In a typical "constellation" by Gomringer, such as the often reproduced "silencio," (1953),[3] the reader must participate in the creation of meaning by unravelling the fused union of semantics and typography. Bayard points out that the missing word "silencio" in the poem has commonly been interpreted as a visual representation of the absence of speech, noise, or sound (New 24). This interpretation is somewhat limited, however, for in addition to reading the poem as a visual analog of silence, one could read the blank space left by the absence of the word "silencio" as a type of noise: silence as information, represented through the graphic "noise" of the blank space. As Michael Riffaterre has argued, poems stem from a repressed matrix of meaning, which does not necessarily need to be present in the text itself. Significance is for Riffaterre "shaped like a doughnut" around the hole of an absent matrix (13). In Gomringer's poem, the presence of a visual "hole" in silence can be read as the generator of either silence, or paradoxically, the absence of silence. Since the text destabilizes the binary opposition between absence and presence, limiting it to a representation of either the presence or the absence of silence is problematic.

Nichol's one word poem "em ty" in *Still Water* (1970)[4] similarly rehearses this type of destabilized binary opposition and assumption of the reader's productive role. For Douglas Barbour, the poem "enacts itself" (33) by calling the reader's attention to the effect of typeset on reading habits. Like Gomringer's theorization of "play activity," Barbour regards the activity of the reader as all important to the production of meaning. And since the presence of emptiness is signified through textual means—i.e. emptiness is graphically rendered through the blank space as signifier—the missing letter p does not miss its destination in the symbolic exchange between text and reader, merely by being absent. If we were to see this missing letter in the shadow of Lacan, we could speculate that it is actually not too far from its aim; the letter always reaches its destination, because its destination turns out to be precisely where it is always already heading: the chain of textual relations in the field of the Other. So Barbour's claim that the poem "enacts itself" is

---

[3]See for example Solt (91) and Williams (n.p.).

[4]*Still Water* is a hinged box containing a group of five inch square leaves of paper, each of which represents an extremely sparse poem (eg. "closedpen / o pen"; "groww"; st*r"). The reader operates this book-machine by shuffling leaves to create random juxtapositions.

instructive, not only in the sense in which he desires to frame the poem,

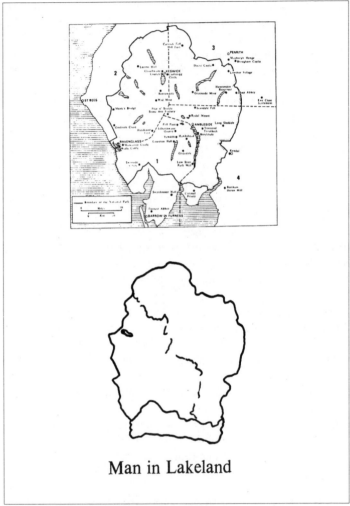

Fig. 4. bpNichol. "Man in Lakeland." 1978. Steve McCaffery and
bpNichol, *In England Now that Spring.*

but also if we consider the poem as an enactment of an em ty frame
through which the Other gazes at us.

The notes on the liner to the Four Horsemen's 1972 *CaNADAda* album of sound poetry emphasize a similar type of double destination between absence and presence: "nada is the Spanish word for nothing & also, in Hindu mythology, for the sound that never ends, the creative principle of the universe." Henderson remarks on the similarities between the Horsemen and Dada: "the variety of sound variation techniques has greatly increased since the Dada poets, but the end is the same: the opening of the self to the energy of the Other" ("Radical" 189). Henderson's Other alternatively signifies community or theological Otherness, and is thus another Other than Lacan's Other. If we were to read Henderson's text psychoanalytically, his Others are closer to Lacan's other (small o), because they function as fantasy substitutes (hence imaginary misrecognitions) for the unattainable. In any case, Henderson's claim that the Horsemen's sound poetry attempts to open the self to communal experience is appropriate, for the *CaNADAda* liner note further states that the sound poem "Seasons" is their "first consciously group conceived, group written composition. At this point the idea of the poem as product of a community starts to become clear to us." The Horsemen's conflation of the three signifiers nada, Dada, and Canada constructs the word "Canada" as a type of multicultural home for numerous dialogical and communal relations, rather than as a monologic concept of national unity.

## 3. De Man in Lakeland
*In England Now that Spring* (1979), a series of "polaroid poems, found texts, visions and collaborations" which Nichol and McCaffery recorded on a journey through England and Scotland in 1978, further illustrates their response to Canadian post-centennial nationalism. Nichol's visual poem "Man in Lakeland" (fig. 4) juxtaposes a drawing of a human face against a map of an English national park in the Lake District; both face and park have the same general contour, and the personified face of the English landscape is facing west, with his gaze fixed across the ocean toward Canada. The detourned[5] idiocy of his look performs in a manner

---

[5]Cf. the Situationist practice of *détournement*—i.e., the deflection, diversion, and appropriation of texts through modifying already existing elements; *détournement* is the "aesthetic occupation of enemy territory, a raid launched to seize the familiar and turn it into the other ... a politics of subversive quotation, of cutting the vocal cords of every empowered speaker" (Marcus 178-79). Guy Debord and the Situationists' politically radical *détournement* of comic strips, advertisements, and maps during the 1950s and 60s would seem to be a significant

that is not unlike the "look" theorized by Jean-Paul Sartre in *Being and Nothingness*. For Sartre, the subject is objectified by the look, although the subject who looks also recognizes that its own look has the potential to be returned. Behind the struggle between the one who looks and the one who is looked at lies the recognition that roles may be reversed, and the object of the look may exercise subjectivity and become the perceiver rather than the perceived. Because the phrenological stupidity of the "Man in Lakeland" illustrates the weakened look of the colonialist Other on its New World offspring, it functions as a reciprocating inversion of traditional colonialist discourses, such as Thomas Cary's 1789 poem *Abram's Plains*, in which "moral [i.e. English] virtues humanize the plain" (l.63).[6] Reversing the typical colonialist humanization of the Canadian landscape, Nichol's poem projects an idiotic facial expression onto the Old World landscape; the "Man in Lakeland" reverses the look's destination from the parental centre to the offspring's periphery.

"Man in Lakeland" presents a *Romantic* image which functions as the Thing that crosses international boundaries. According to Paul De Man, Wordsworth's description of the descent of the Simplon Pass in *Book VI* of *The Prelude* "describes the passage from a certain type of nature, earthly and material, to another nature which could be called mental and celestial" (13). This shift is first marked in Wordsworth by the use of oxymorons, such as "the stationary blast of waterfalls," and is then followed by a move toward a non-terrestrial nature that is "associated with the diaphanous, limpid, and immaterial quality of a light that dwells nearer to the skies" (14). While Nichol's visual poem does not allude to this sort of immaterial light, it conflates the irreconcilable opposites of human face and landscape, thereby dis-figuring each term, and setting up the type of catachresis that De Man finds in *The Prelude*. To re-contextualize De Man's words on Wordsworth, the setting of the "Man in

---

pre-text for the TRG's appropriations, although the Group do not mention any Situationist texts in their list of jointly discussed readings from 1972 to approximately 1984 (*Rational* 313-320). See Ken Knabb, ed. *International Situationist Anthology* (1981), and Susan Sussman, ed. *on the passage of a few people through a rather brief moment in time: THE SITUATIONIST INTERNATIONAL 1957-1968* (1989).

[6]See D.M.R. Bentley's 1986 introduction to *Abram's Plains: A Poem* for a discussion of the colonialist desire to humanize the Quebec landscape.

Lakeland" is located "somewhere between the inaccessible mountain peaks and the humanized world of the plains; it is a deeply divided and paradoxical nature that, in Rousseau's terms, 'seems to take pleasure in self-opposition'" (13-14). Moreover, the poem that immediately follows the "Man in Lakeland," entitled "In Lakeland," further follows Wordsworth by constructing nature as the sign for a spiritualized reality: "the mouth of the Deep level // as near as we may safely come to / the actual" (n.p.). Nichol does not define or describe his "Deep level," except to objectify it as a body of water and/or to personify it by giving it a mouth, and readers are left to wonder if it refers to an object such as a river or ocean or to a state of consciousness. J. Hillis Miller's definition of catachresis is useful in this context: "the forced or abusive transfer of terms from an alien realm to name something which has no proper name in itself since it is not an object which can be confronted by the senses" (21); the catachresis of the "Deep level" with a mouth offers us the illusion of a meaning that could never be actualized as a presence, outside of figuration. Thus, the image functions in a similar manner to De Man's description of a non-terrestrial, "mental" object which puts into question the ontological priority of the sensory object. The poem exhibits a desire (or in De Man's terms, an intentional structure) for the em ty nothing that could never become a particularized object. In terms adopted by Žižek after Lacan, the enjoyment of that nothingness as materialized Thing *qua* "Deep level" or dis-figured facial landscape operates as the necessary condition for maintaining symbolic coherence. In other words, Nichol's construction of "immaterial" poetic images reinforces a specific social order's imaginary relationship to the material conditions of existence, because these images serve as a site for enjoyment in response to the lack that constitutes subjectivity.

*4. "We are writing this book as a rhizome. It is composed of plateaus. We have given it a circular form, but only for laughs."*
Shortly after the publication of *In England Now That Spring*, the League of Canadian Poets published a pamphlet by McCaffery entitled *The Scenarios* (1980). The text consists of a series of notes for performance events, similar to the early Dadaist performances held at the Cabaret Voltaire in Zurich during the first world war. For example: "a man sits on a mountain slope wearing a postcard / almost three hours pass until he sticks a stamp onto the mountain side." Much like the dis-figured facial landscape of the "Man in Lakeland," the physical environment in this scenario is a letter, a text subject to a chain of relations in the Other. On

the back of the pamphlet, McCaffery claims that his favourite Canadian poets are Margaret Avison and Marcel Duchamp. This playful mistake sets up a rhizomatic connection between international and national categories by collapsing its own terms of reference. For Deleuze and Guattari, a rhizome "pertains to a map that must be produced, constructed, a map that is always detachable, connectable, reversible, modifiable" (*Thousand* 21);[B] McCaffery's map erases the lines between nations by situating Duchamp, a French artist who lived much of his life in New York, in the context of Canadian poetry. The text thus places the League of Canadian Poets in league with multiplicities. Perhaps McCaffery is mistaken when he writes about a man sitting on a *mountain* wearing a postcard, for the mountain is extremely similar to a *plateau* which mutates into a letter-machine ("We call a 'plateau' any multiplicity connected to other multiplicities by superficial underground stems in such a way as to form a rhizome" [*Thousand* 22]).

McCaffery's rhizomatic writing illustrates how the word "Canada" might function as a site for literary dispute, for if we consider at all seriously the implications of Gomringer's invitation to the reader to produce the poem's meaning—an implication which is consistent with McCaffery's project[EE]—the notion of a national literature becomes highly questionable. If a Canadian reader produces the poem's meaning, is the poem a "Canadian" text? My reading of Dante, for example, constructs a Canadian inferno, because I can imagine the ice at the lowest circle of Hell far more clearly than I can imagine the forests of Tuscany. "Canada" in McCaffery's work is not the type of authoritative word that is located in a distanced and untouchable zone, but is instead the site for an ongoing re-interpretive process.

# Derrida

## 1. Macrosyntax

In "Rational Geomancy: A Realignment of Kinships" (1978), the TRG assert that since the appearance of Derrida's grammatology "writing has developed into a giant domain inclusive of a number of previously scattered disciplines" (*Rational* 154). As a "macrosyntactic unit," they write, "all literature is seen[7] as one huge, spherical sentence, continuously expanding, whose grammar and arrangement is continuously permutated and modified" (155). This visual sentence is riddled with an "infinite" number of reading paths (156). Because these paths assume a multiplicity of possible and potentially contradictory readings based on the unlimited number of traces in the macrosyntactic context, they rehearse Derrida's critique of self-presence in relation to the differential traces of writing. Moreover, by reconfiguring writing as a reorganization of "patterns we perceive in literature" (153), the Group further follows Derrida's practice

---

[7]Ironically, the visuality of the TRG's literary sphere (the fact that they *see* this sphere) is subject to the same type of critique that Derrida offers to the Western philosophical tradition—i.e., that the tenor of the dominant metaphor in philosophy always returns to the "major signified of ontotheology: the circle of the heliotrope" ("White" 266). For Derrida, the circular metaphor: "has marked not only Platonic, Aristotelian, Cartesian, and other kinds of discourse, not only the science of logic as the circle of circles, but also, and by the same token, the man of metaphysics. The sensory sun, which rises in the East, becomes interiorized, in the evening of its journey, in the eye and the heart of the Westerner. He summarizes, assumes, and achieves the essence of man, 'illuminated by the true light'" ("White" 268). Even though the TRG follow Derrida by aligning grammatology with "a giant domain [of writing] inclusive of a number of previously scattered disciplines," their vision of a literary sphere continues the heliocentric tradition that is the object of Derrida's critique. If, as Derrida suggests, the heliocentric metaphor illuminates the unified subject of metaphysics, the Group's use of that metaphor deconstructs their desire to represent writing as a dis-unified multiplicity, in which "the writer can never know the entire macrosyntactic context from which her readers draw" (157).

of dismantling the hierarchichal oppositons between binary terms. In their account, writing *is* reading, and vice versa.

The TRG's rehearsal of Derridean concepts calls into question commonly held beliefs about the writing process, such as the valorization of originality and the authenticity of the expressive speaking voice. At the risk of producing yet another deconstructive reading of *The Martyrology*, it is important to point out the influence of these Derridean perspectives on Nichol's long poem, and to illustrate the extent to which his text sidesteps its own engagement with Derrida. Nichol was exposed to Derrida through his collaborative work with McCaffery shortly after the publication of *Book 2* in 1972; Scobie claims that *Book 3*'s "CODA: Mid-Initial Sequence" is "key to the development of the whole poem," because it shifts away from the text's earlier mythological visions towards the "free play of dissemination, the deconstruction of the word throughout Books 4 and 5 ("Surviving" 65). After describing an image of two poets who "disagreed," Nichol writes: "d is a greed / a gluttony of shape / swallowing the era which it ends / discorporates." On one hand, the charade[P] between "disagreed" and "d is a greed" foregrounds grammatology over phonocentrism, because the phonocentric speaker is literally taken out of the body (discorporated) and swallowed by the textual Other. The end of the phonocentric era is thus synonymous to the death of the saints and the failure of language mourned by the narrator of the first two books. On the other hand, however, *The Martyrology*'s specific form of notation re-incorporates the body, thereby limiting the disseminative free-play of the signifier. In a 1985 interview with Daphne Marlatt and George Bowering, Nichol claimed: "when you're trying to notate your breath, what you're going to get is the syntax of your body" ("Syntax" 32), and he includes the statement "all spacing in *The Martyrology* is deliberate" at the end of *Book 6 Books*. The controlling pause signalled by every line end
as well as with      in lines, ensures that the text does not entirely detach writing from the body of a speaking or listening subject.[N] The latter books of *The Martyrology* uphold a grammatological "alphabet / A to Z of / being" (*Book 4*), while simultaneously setting up an indeterminate interchange of textuality and bodily experience. In effect, the poem's notational tactics reveal the body to be text, thereby rehearsing a type of Derridean invagination; for Derrida, invagination is the "inverted reapplication of the outer edge to the inside of a form where the outside then opens a pocket" ("Living" 97). In Nichol's text, body-notation

functions as a pocket which enfolds the external Other, which in turn enfolds the body, and so on ad infinitum. While the charade differentiates writing from speech, Nichol's deconstruction of the border between writing and speech, through "body syntax," foregrounds *The Martyrology*'s deconstructive poetics—i.e., the inscription of a body in language, where both speech and writing are constructed simultaneously as central and marginal.

## 2. Supper's Ready

While commentators such as Stephen Scobie, Frank Davey, and Smaro Kamboureli have emphasized the important influence of Derrida's writing on *The Martyrology*, the relationship between the body and the Derridean concepts that run throughout the text has been largely overlooked. In fact, the complex inscription of the body as text is central to the poem, and can be charted from the lyrical representation of an abject body in the early books, towards the deconstructive blurring of body and text in the middle and latter books. For example, *Book 1* is frequently marked by abject images, such as the narrator's claim: "i throw up these poems ... out of the moment of the soul's searching." "Food loathing," writes Julia Kristeva in *Powers of Horror* (1980) "is perhaps the most elementary and most archaic form of abjection" (2). To abject is to expel the undefinable and horrific object that lacks clear conceptual boundaries, and abject material is the other that is cast out by the subject in order to constitute a bounded ego. Abjection is symptomatic of the horror and violent expulsion of the liminal space between inside and outside; Kristeva writes that the body abjects its inside—its urine, blood, vomit, and excrement—"in order to compensate for the collapse of the border between inside and outside" (53). In *Book 1*, Saint Reat goes on a quest for "the origins of all voice." Expressing a sense of horror and despair at his painful isolation, and at his failure to reach the origin of language "with all speech gone," Saint Reat spews out abject images:

> tumble tongue   fish face
> sayer of dreams
>
> comer in nightmares
> screaming & babbling
>
> slime nose and green lip
>
> dribbler of phrases
> symbols & spewing

blood cougher swamp dweller 'loon'

This horror reaches a peak in the chant near the end of *Book 2* (1972), a section that Scobie claims is *The Martyrology*'s most anguished statement of isolation: "no chain of words to bind you to me / how can I live who cannot be without you / knowing you are dead you are dead you are dead dead dead." Scobie argues that the early books of *The Martyrology* are "haunted by this fear of the death of the saints, of the failure of language" (*bpNichol* 117).

As we have seen, *Book 3*'s publication after Nichol's exposure to Derrida illustrates how its narrator has come to terms with the abjection and failure of representation that is expressed in the first two books. *Book 3* further departs from portraying an isolated self, and turns instead to representing communal relationships. The text begins with a list of food ("carrots onions celery potatoes / cheddar cheese / beef or stock") and the eating of a communal meal ("sit around the table / talk of nothing / good feeling for the job that's done"). For Davey, the passage "finds the writer in the clarity of a domestic ritual, the words directly projecting the actuality of the body's condition: food as sustenance and as substance of the communal" (20). Instead of the earlier abject food loathing which signifies subjective isolation and the failure of language, the narrator of *Book 3* loses his sense of separation and regains his appetite; he begins to eat his way through the communally shared alphabet.

Although the dramatic shift in tone from horrific despair to playful celebration that occurs in the third book occurs alongside of Nichol's negotiation of the speech/writing binary, the indeterminacy of the relationship between inside and outside does not provoke the sort of abject response found in the earlier books. By *Book 5, Chain 7*, for example, Nichol re-writes the abject imagery from *Book 1* quoted above in the form of a play, where the chorus speaks: "tumble tongue, fish face, sayer of dreams. comer in nightmares screaming & babbling. slime nose & green lip, dribbler of phrases, symbols & spewing. blood cougher, swamp dweller, loon." Instead of the lyric voice of *Book 1*, Nichol recasts this section as a dramatic dialogue. For Clint Burnham, the direct quotations taken from *Book 1* become "spoken representations of a written text (speech represents writing)" (207). Yet because this part of *Chain 7* is the written *script* of a play, Burnham's interpretation is somewhat problematic. *Chain 7* is not only the spoken representation of a written text—it is also the written representation of a spoken text (writing represents speech). Moreover, this indeterminate relationship between spoken and written texts stems from an intertextual recasting of an earlier writing. As Kristeva points out, intertextuality is not merely the search for original sources, rather, it "situates the text within history and society, which are then seen as texts read by the writer, and into which he inserts himself by rewriting them" (*Desire* 65).[1] Nichol's re-situation of the single speaking subject's discourse from *Book 1*, into the shared social context of the chorus's discourse in *Book 5*, seems to recontextualize abject images as images of carnivalesque celebration, in which Apollo puts on the mask of Dionysus, and parties with the chorus: "every(allat(toge(forever)ther)once)thing" (*Chain 10*).

This carnivalesque celebraton of the dissemination of language does not necessarily imply that Nichol's longpoem is entirely indebted to Derrida, for *The Martyrology's* inscription of a speaking 'I', along with its use of journalistic form[U], recuperates a self-present subject at the thematic level. The text formally problematizes the difference between body and writing, letter and word, yet its continual return to the lyric voice counters the radical implications of Derrida's critique of logocentrism.[Q] Nichol's longpoem offers readers the comforting assurances of a de-politicized, atheoretical humanism that is only partially de-stabilized by the ramifications of its own formal procedures.

# Excess Expenditure

## 1. Bifurcations

In the TRG's 1981 discussion of the synaesthesial demand of scratch 'n' sniff books,[8] McCaffery asks the question: "does the text exist or is it transformed by these mechanics into loss and discharge?" (*Rational* 176).[B] His concern with expenditure is more fully developed in essays written apart from the TRG, however, such as in "Language Writing: From Productive to Libidinal Economy" (1980), where he quotes Georges Bataille: "Communication, in my sense of the word, is never stronger than when communication, in the weak sense of profane language ... fails and becomes the equivalent of darkness" (qtd. in McCaffery 156). Since sovereign communication is radically unproductive, it is heterogeneous to social homogeneity. As Martin Jay observes, Bataille contended that sovereign communication demands obscurity because it challenges lucid prose as a "clear passage of ideas from one subjectivity to another" (230). Following Emile Durkheim's characterization of the "*sacred*" as anything that is absolutely heterogeneous to the profane, Bataille writes that the heterogeneous world includes everything resulting from *unproductive expenditure*, and consists of everything that is rejected by homogeneous society as either refuse *or* as superior transcendent value. Bataille's version of the sacred is not to be understood as a theological legitimation of a deity, but in the sense of incommensurate otherness. In *Literature and Evil* (1957; trans. 1973) he writes that sovereign communication can only occur when "we resort to evil, that is to say the violation of the law" (172). As a sacred and evil "(*non*)discourse," sovereign communication attempts to expend meaning and de-legitimate the transmission of knowledge as a support for the self-

---

[8]Scratch 'n' sniff books invite readers to "scratch the page, thereby releasing the odour of the printed signified" (*Rational* 176). The TRG mention this form of literature in the context of their discussion of innovative book-machines.

conscious subject.

Because of sovereign communication's capacity to violate the law, McCaffery imbricates Bataille's general economy with a psychoanalytically based theory of libidinal economy:

The major premise in libidinal economy is that language is possessed of a double disposition: one towards naming, logicalizing, predicating; the other towards an assertion of pre-linguistic gestures (what Kristeva has termed the semiotic order) that push through but remain attached to symbolic meaning (*North* 154).[9]

---

[9]McCaffery does not directly cite Jean-François Lyotard's *Libidinal Economy* (1974; trans. 1993) in "Language Writing: From Productive to Libidinal Economy," although both texts politicize psychoanalysis. Lyotard's text is extremely resistant to paraphrase due to its delirious construction of an unsublatable dichotomy between, on the one hand, logical concepts, and on the other hand, opaque disruptions of meaning which violate the limits of communicable knowledge. A typical example: "[f]ar from taking the great Zero [Ian Hamilton Grant glosses the "great Zero" as "a general term to cover the Platonic world of forms, God, the authentic mode of production, the phallus, etc." [xii]) as the ontological motif, imposed on desire, forever deferring, re-presenting and simulating everything in an endless postponement, we, libidinal economists, affirm that this zero is itself a figure, part of a powerful *dispositif*, wise like the god of the Jews and pale like the void of Lao-tzu, a concentratory *dispositif* [*dispositif de circonversion*] where, of course, several libidinal positions are affirmed together, which we make merry in disintricating and demonstrating with tact, in disengaging without shock, like Japanese, like blades enmeshed in a fencing match—and we will show not only that it is necessary to pass through it in order to follow the course of intensities on the labyrinth, but moreover that the passage through the zero is itself a particular libidinal course, that the position of the signifier or of the Other is, in the contradictory *dispositif*, itself an enjoyable [*jouissive*] position, that the 'rigour of the law' gives more than one person a hard-on, and that this Nothing is not a matter of ontological necessity, but of a religious fantasy, libidinal then, and as such, moreover, quite acceptable, that is, if it were not, alas, terroristic and deontic" (5). The structure and content of this sentence—its length, its numerous clauses, its allusiveness, its deferrals— performs an economic interchange between the transmission of discursive content and the principle of interruption. These two categories do not structure the text by operating as mutually exclusive binaries. Rather, they mutually inform each other in an economic exchange—an economy that Lyotard regards as "libidinal" because it evokes "intensities ... unbound excitations of force which are characterized by their displaceability, their instantaneity and their resistance to the temporal synthesis of memory" (Grant xiii). While McCaffery calls for this type

McCaffery's version of unruly libidinal economy explicitly recalls Kristeva's early theory of subjectivity-as-process, split between an interchange of conscious and unconscious categories. Kristeva posits a division between presocial semiotic drives, which she associates with the maternal body, and the grammatical and social constraints of the symbolic order. Existing as a residue of gaps, contradictions and pulsions in language, semiotic disruption adopts the "dream logic, it transgresses rules of linguistic code and social morality" (*Desire* 70).

In a 1984 interview with Andrew Payne, McCaffery places critical importance on the dialectical character of Kristeva's subject-in-process:

Part bound, part articulated by a verbal order (the self of the proper name, the name of the Father in the son) and yet incessantly . . . ruptured by instinctual drives that surge through the linguistic order and are felt in (but never identified as) rhythm, intonation (*North* 128).

Defining libidinal economy as a double-disposition between the logic of the symbolic order and pre-linguistic semiotic gestures, McCaffery specifies that libidinal economy is "politics beyond politics" (*North* 153), and constructs a structural analogy between general economy's challenge to the politics of productive use-value and the semiotic order's disruption of the unicity of the symbolic order. McCaffery's reading of Kristeva therefore does not support an essentialist, a-historical mode of being, rather, it is consistent with Marilyn Edelstein's argument that the Kristevan subject is created "in and through language, at the place where the word and flesh meet, and since language is a social practice, the subject and the social cannot be separated" (204). Because the semiotic is fundamentally at odds with the symbolic, the relation between the two categories produces a split subject, thereby unsettling the symbolic order's

---

of double disposition in his essay on libidinal economy and Language Writing, his text stresses the relationship between conceptual and figurative categories in a language which is relatively devoid of the disruptions found in Lyotard's *Libidinal Economy* (eg. Language Writing "exposes the fetishization of the linguistic sign by ideological constraint that brings the linguistic order disturbingly close to that of the political order" [*North* 152]). Despite the fact that Lyotard's text precedes McCaffery's essay, McCaffery neglects Lyotard, and explicitly centres on Kristeva and Bataille.

claims to ideological totalization.[10] General and libidinal economies both problematize the ideological legitimation of stable, grammatically and representationally transmitted knowledge between subjects, and both categories question the ideological principle of social homogeneity. For Bataille, homogeneous knowledge is structured on identity and science, while heterogeneous knowledge is identical to the structure of the unconscious, and can only be represented as "something *other*, as *incommensurate*, by charging these words with the *positive* value they have in *affective* experience" (*Visions* 143). Bataille further argues that the exclusion of impure heterogeneity from homogeneous society formally recalls the exclusion of the unconscious from the conscious psyche in psychoanalysis (141). Yet social homogeneity and heterogeneity are bound together, for homogenous society normalizes itself and gains stability through destructive sadism directed toward external and internal elements, such as a foreign other or an impoverished class. Because the exclusion of these heterogeneous elements is the pre-condition for social homogeneity, both homogeneity and heterogeneity are dialectically related. Similarly, the heterogeneous Kristevan semiotic is imbricated with the seeming homogeneity of symbolic logic and order, and the split-subject-in-process exists as an unfinalizable contradiction between two

---

[10]McCaffery cites Kristeva's *Desire in Language* (1980) and *Revolution in Poetic Language* (1984) as precedents to his discussion of the political link between libidinal and general economy (*North* 154). In the former text, Kristeva argues that the symbolic function of language constitutes itself through the repression of instinctual drive and the subject's incestuous relation to the mother, while poetic language reactivates this repressed maternal element. She refers to Bataille's *Literature and Evil* as a pre-text for her discussion of the symbolic order's taboo against incest: "because it utters incest, poetic language is linked with 'evil'" (137). Poetic language is the equivalent of incest, for unlike the constitution of the subject through difference at the Oedipal stage (i.e. its acquisition of language and entrance "into" the symbolic order), semiotic activity reveals the word as never *uniquely* a sign of difference. Archaic pulsions stem from the semiotic body and reside in the poetic word, ensuring that the subject is never completely separate from its pre-Oedipal and incestuous identification with the mother. In *Revolution in Poetic Language*, Kristeva further claims that Bataille's writing "moves beyond madness and realism in a leap that maintains both 'delirium' and 'logic'" (82)—in other words, Bataille's writing is an explicit realization of the subject-in-process *qua* split between the semiotic / symbolic dialectic.

irreconcilable elements. In effect, this dialectical relationship provides a challenge to the logic of ideological totalization and is for Kristeva the precondition of subjectivity.

Although McCaffery adopts Bataille's and Kristeva's writings as theoretical pre-texts, he asserts that Language writing is not solely sovereign, unproductive, semiotic. On the one hand, Language writing petitions active productive engagement on the part of the reader. In this mode the text is "viewed as a game affording both author and reader the possibility of producing endless meanings and relationships" (Mistacco qtd. in *North* 149). As in the Barthesian "writerly" text, McCaffery here assumes a reader who is not a passive consumer but an active producer of meaning. Citing Barthes' *S/Z* (1974), McCaffery claims the writerly text is indeterminate to the extent that it: "is resistant to habitual reading; it is 'the novelistic without the novel, poetry without the poem ... production without product' making the reader no longer a consumer but a producer of the text" (*North* 143). In this productive mode, McCaffery calls for a destabilized relationship between signifier and signified, thereby de-stabilizing the author/reader relationship, which he regards as analogous to the producer/consumer relationship. On the other hand, however, McCaffery proposes reading through general and libidinal economies. As a general economy of semiotic excess, Language writing celebrates the death of conventional meaning and overturns the principle of rational communication between self-conscious subjects. Instead of pointing to multivalent and indeterminate meanings which are produced by the reader rather than the writer, general economy expends representationally governed meaning. McCaffery refuses to privilege these hermeneutic procedures, and claims that both strategies of reading are simultaneously called for by Language writing: "it should be possible within these texts to institute a double rhythm of reading: utilitarian-productive and non-utilitarian resistant and to allow their interaction and mutual relativization *inside a dialectical economy*" (*North* 158). By proposing that Language writing provides the reader with an unsublatable opposition between productive utility and libidinal sovereignty, McCaffery questions the subject's attachment to unified meaning as a guarantee of self-conscious-ness.

## 2. Swift and/or Bataille

McCaffery's *The Black Debt* (1989) is a diptych formed between two long pieces entitled "Lag" and "An Effect of Cellophane." The text is printed in large boldface letters with justified margins on both sides. "Lag," consists of a series of disjunctive propositions divided solely by commas: "... icons in an age of accuracy by glass, it's happening in the past, concrete unfolding into signified precision ..." (56). "An Effect of Cellophane" abandons punctuation altogether in favour of a discontinuous stream of linguistic combinations drawn from a finite vocabulary: "... spherical the sphere a page that burns a charred appeal to fresco limned but limited sometimes body contrary classic ..." (141). For Marjorie Perloff, the writing presents an "information overload" that criticizes commercial advertising discourses through the ironic evocation of signboards, tickertape, and electronic mail (*Radical* 104-11). Reading *The Black Debt* for its satirical reworking of mass-media material, she constructs McCaffery as a latter-day Jonathan Swift who must fictionalize his materials in order to represent the "true horror and absurdity" of contemporary commercial discourse (110). Her interpretation situates the text within a canonically established genre. But because this genre historically criticizes social aberrations from the standpoint of a desirable norm, Perloff's reading unconsciously justifies the type of rigid binary opposition (abberation/norm, ignorance/knowledge, truth/falsehood) that McCaffery calls into question through his legitimation of Bataille's general economy and Kristeva's subject-in-process. For McCaffery Bataillian expenditure attacks the bar between antithetical terms, and is an operation "entirely devoid of self-interest and whose direction is towards break-down and discharge rather than accumulation and integration" (*North* 213). General economy dissolves binary terms as separate identities and libidinal economy blurs (rather than separates) symbolic and semiotic registers.

Perloff cites the opening lines of "Lag": "SENTENCE NOT SEN-TENCE, A RED envelope, the rain stood up, the prolonged cosseting or a silhouette the customer knows, dead drunks arriving at a gate" (*Black* 11; qtd. in Perloff 106). She reads the first phrase, "SENTENCE NOT SENTENCE," as both a self-reflexive statement of aesthetics and a pun on the unconventional writing that the reader is "sentenced" to read (*Radical* 107). Her interpretation implicitly foregrounds a Barthesian "writerly" reading strategy inasmuch as it produces meaning, rather than unproblematically receiving meaning through the transmission of a stable message from writer to reader. Treating each of the phrases reproduced above in terms of their capacity to produce multivalent meaning, she further suggests that the hermeneutic "lag" of McCaffery's satirical wordplay forces delay, thereby producing for readers a site for perception about vulnerability to "prefabricated messages" and "bogus claims to authority" (111). Perloff constructs the text in terms of its capacity to *produce* a politically *useful* meaning for Marxism through its critique of commodity culture. In other words, she constructs a critical paraphrase of the radical *theme* of the text—i.e. its challenge to mass media—thereby limiting the text to a single meaning while avoiding its capacity to exceed and deterritorialize any instrumental purpose. Her thematic criticism falls into the category of Barthesian "metalanguage"; following Bataille, Barthes claims that the contradictory text:

> liquidates all metalanguage ... no voice (Science, Cause, Institution) is *behind* what it is saying. Next, the text destroys utterly, *to the point of contradiction*, its own discursive category, its sociolinguistic reference (its 'genre'): 'it is the comical that does not make us laugh' (*Pleasure* 30).

Perloff's interpretation is certainly feasible at the conceptual level, because *The Black Debt* does indeed question syntactical and semantic conventions while offering readers the opportunity to produce meanings. However, her work could be augmented by pointing out that any reduction of the text to a critique of mediaspeak recuperates its ambivalent inscription of affect, its "black debt" to the gleeful horrors of irresolution, comedic disgust, and the trans-instrumental.

If the text refuses interpretation, how do we read it? Kristeva metaphorically compares the unsettling effect of poetic language with social revolution's disruptive effect on political order, and McCaffery employs Kristevan theory precisely because it allows him a means to theorize the "unreadable" text as "a break-down of social code and the eruption of a radical otherness within the linguistic order" ("Unreadable" 220). This radical otherness occurs not only through the writerly production of variant symbolic meanings, but also through the disruption of the symbolic by "a language always in excess of its verbal, discursive form and carrying the logically anterior energies that do not define so much as 'mark' the movement of the self as a plurality of desires" (220-21). For "logically anterior energies" read *affect*—i.e., the missing component in a purely conceptual situation of text as the vehicle for a reader's production of semantics. The double rhythm that is offered to readers by McCaffery's theory sidesteps interpretive recuperation, because it suspends the desire for meaning *qua* object in an endless oscillation between acceptance and rejection. His early consideration of Kristevan poetics[K/L] could therefore be further developed in the light of Kristeva's *Powers of Horror*. Reading at the interstices between restricted and general economies provokes the type of affective ambivalence described by Kristeva as an "apocalyptic laughter," an exclamation of horror, a prophetic laughter that has no morality to defend. Kristeva describes this laughter as the "black mysticism of transcendental collapse" and the "gushing forth of an unconscious ... neither jovial, nor trustful, nor sublime, nor enraptured by preexisting harmony. It is bare, anguished, and as fascinated as it is frightened" (206). McCaffery's black laughter expends the social order, not only by providing readers with a site for the examination of writing as the scene of claims about truth and falsehood, but also by relativizing that site in a dialectical economy of expenditure and production. The differential tension existing among *The Black Debt*'s proliferation of phrasal units suggests a "politics beyond politics," for it agitates the grammatical and nominal formats of power and knowledge, while simultaneously rehearsing a loss reconstituted as textual expansion.

# $F$ootnote

---

As to the footnote, we had been made aware of its dialectical potential by Fredric Jameson,[11] who promotes it to the status of a minor genre (*Rational* 14).

In the introduction to *Rational Geomancy* McCaffery notes that he and Nichol had initially planned to instigate a dialogue between the early reports and a series of contemporary footnotes. These notes were intended to provoke thought about "change and fixity across typographic time" (14). However, their plan could not be carried out because of Nichol's death, and McCaffery writes that he decided to revise the style of the reports, while leaving their content intact. Yet one notable exception occurs in the footnote to their early report "Some Notes on Jerome Rothenberg and Total Translation" (1975), where McCaffery revises the text by adding comments written after the report was first published. The report upholds Rothenberg's translations of Native oral poetry in *Shaking*

---

[11]McCaffery cites a lengthy passage from Jameson's *Marxism and Form* (1971): "The footnote in this context may indeed be thought of as a small but autonomous *form*, with its own inner laws and conventions and its own determinate relationship to the larger form which governs it.... The very limits of the footnote (it must be short, it must be complete) allow the release of intellectual energies, in that they serve as a check on the speculative tendency that might otherwise run wild.... The footnote as such, therefore, designates a moment in which systematic philosophizing and the empirical study of concrete phenomena are both false in themselves; in which living thought, squeezed out from between them, pursues its fitful existence in the small print at the bottom of the page" (qtd. in *Rational* 14). Jameson's comments invite us to question whether or not the relationship between a footnote and the body of a text is symmetrical—i.e., whether or not one has as much "value" as the other. Recent discursive frames of reference as diverse as psychoanalysis, deconstruction, and New Historicism invest marginal remarks of seemingly little significance with critical importance.

*the Pumpkin* (1972), which the TRG claim "sanctions translation as a collaborative and trans-disciplinary act, a gesture across race, cultures, times, and individuals" (*Rational* 51).[12] Rothenberg translates the Senecan "Shaking the Pumpkin" into a visual "equivalent," which the TRG dehistoricize by suggesting that it "exists absolutely in the present without recourse to the historical contextuality of the past":

```
T                           H E H E H H E H
h
e                           H E H E H H E H

The animals are coming by   H E H E H H E H
n
i                           H E H E H H E H
m
a                           H E H E H H E H
l
s
```

(qtd. in *Rational* 48).

Rothenberg's ethnopoetics attempts to think outside the boundaries of Western literature by considering non-literate forms such as song, speech, and the breath. But by translating Native songs into concrete poems, he follows a typically modernist appropriation of non-Western forms of cultural expression. The TRG follow this legitimation, for they construct Rothenberg's texts as a means to:

reinforce the growing sense that 'primitive' equals 'modern,' that so much twentieth-century investigation in the arts has led to: the rediscovery of roots, to a re-establishment of the past within the current, and the presidential belief that all history is contemporaneous (*Rational* 51).

Nichol and McCaffery refer to Western modernist artists who were interested in non-Western art forms, not because of these forms' function in the cultures where they had been made, but simply because of the innovative ways in which their makers had dealt with certain aesthetic problems. Many of the oral narratives collected and translated in Rothenberg's texts were not considered as aesthetic commodities in their traditional social contexts, but as ritual songs or sacred histories. The

---

[12]Rothenberg is not only an editor and translator of Native poetry; he has also translated Eugen Gomringer into English.

introduction of these texts into modernist aesthetic discourses changed their meaning and function; by aligning their own project with the metamorphosized poetry in *Shaking the Pumpkin*, the TRG legitimate the Western appropriation of Native texts.

This early TRG report presents a typical counter-culture blending of ideological difference. Davey comments that the "youth" culture of the 1960s and early 70s attempted to elide boundaries among different political agendas in favour of a common struggle against the "establish-ment" within a general "paradigm of youth and age" (*Canadian* 12-13). Members of visible minorities such as Michael Ondaatje and Fred Wah "constructed themselves, and were constructed by readers, through the available discourses of youth, avant-gardism, and anti-instrumentalism" (Davey 13). The TRG's 1973 report on Rothenberg's translation fits neatly into this paradigm, for it blurs the ideological differences between avant-gardism and Native issues.

In the 1992 footnote to this report, however, McCaffery revises the text by writing:

We were never entirely satisfied with this interim report. Most especially we developed reservations around the trans-historic values being proposed. While valorizing the leap across historic partition we also realized and believed that any creative act participates and enters into the complex historic process of social and productive forces that we simplify as "now" (Rational 53).

Although McCaffery claims that the TRG had "reservations" about trans-historic values, these reservations were not represented in the early report. But by the 90s, McCaffery no longer justifies the notion that all of history is contemporaneous. Moreover, the footnote further cites his "Anti-Phonies: Fred Wah's *Pictograms from the Interior of B.C.*," which discusses the "complicity between translation and ethnology." These revisions illustrate a desire to move away from elided difference toward ideological specificity—a desire which aligns the text with a number of contemporary discourses supporting minority issues and marginalized cultures.

The appropriation of a different symbolic organization that is assumed by the TRG in the first version of the report is also an expression of desire for a different relationship toward enjoyment. As we have seen, Žižek argues that a cultural group can exist only when its specific enjoyment is materialized through social practices, and transmitted through myths that structure these practices.[c] By justifying the use of Native social practices in a modernist aesthetic context, the early TRG uphold the modernist myth of trans-historic and trans-cultural value, thereby stimulating Western enjoyment. However, this modernist enjoyment is complicit with the type of colonialist appropriations that threaten Native access to their own specific social practice and enjoyment. McCaffery's later footnote problematizes—but does not forget—this modernist desire for the non-Western Other's enjoyment. If the text had been omitted from the collection, or if it had been re-written entirely from the perspective of a post-colonial challenge to the modernist ideology assumed by the earlier version, it would be far less accurate about its own role in the colonialist project. Instead, the footnote dialogizes the earlier text by illustrating its compliance with the Western seizure of Native cultural artifacts. One could of course argue that McCaffery's relegation of this critique to a footnote diminishes its importance, thereby maintaining the hierarchy that it seeks to displace. On the other hand, however, McCaffery follows Jameson's construction of the footnote as an "autonomous form" in which "living thought" is "squeezed out" from between "systematic philosophizing and the empirical study of concrete phenomena" (qtd. in *Rational* 14), and the "living thought" of his later re-vision calls into question the earlier text's appropriative strategy, because it acknowledges the history of Western dominance in North America.[13] The footnote's criticism of trans-historic values in the 1992 version of the essay implies that the Western enjoyment of its own cultural practices should only occur in relation to the Other's access to its own enjoyment, and not at the Other's expense. As a "minor genre," the footnote supplements the 1975 text to construct cultural enjoyment as a dialogic relationship of difference, instead of as a homogenous aesthetic project under the sign of avant-gardism.

---

[13]For this reason, the footnote is sympathetic to Native author Beth Brant's call for non-Native representations of Native/Western relationships: "I do not say that only Indians can write about Indians. But you [the West] can't steal my stories and call them your own. This is the history of North America—stolen property, stolen lives, stolen dreams, stolen spirituality. If your history is one of cultural dominance you must be aware and truthful about that history. You must *own* that history before you can get permission to write about me.... You have to tell the truth and that means you have to tell the truth about *your* role, *your* history, *your* internalized domination and supremacy" (12).

# Geomancy

## 1. Natural Language

Geomancy took the existing elements in nature, aligning and shaping them to augment and focus the yin/yang energy currents that flow over the earth's surface. Geomancy and geomantic translation are both activities in which the central act is the realignment of space and of the balance between already existing phenomenon [sic] (*Rational* 33). *Geomancy* is defined as 'the art of divination by means of signs, derived from the earth, as by the figure assumed by a handful of earth thrown down upon some surface.Hence, usually divination by means of lines or figures formed by jotting down on paper a number of dots at random' (OED qtd. in *Rational* 153).

The TRG's 1973 remarks on geomancy and geomantic translation are consistent with their continual stress on the signifier's materiality. By constructing an analogy between on the one hand the magical art of geomancy "as practised in ancient China and by the lost builders of stonehenge" (*Rational* 33), and on the other hand the graphic organization of marks on a page, their report supports a nostalgic desire for original presence. As Bayard points out, this desire is typically present in both isomorphic and constructivist concrete discourses.[14] Citing Foucault's *The Order of Things*, (1966; trans. 1971), Bayard aligns the isomorphic concretists' attempt to fuse form and content with the pre-Cartesian episteme's correlation of all things, where language is merely one element in a mirror-world of duplication and analogy. Foucault considers language in the pre-Cartesian episteme to possess a symbolic function only in its "total relation to the totality of the world, in the intersecting of its space with the loci and forms of the cosmos" (*Order* 37). Conversely, Bayard

---

[14]During the late 1950s and early 60s, a debate emerged between isomorphic concretists who fused meaning and visual design and constructivist concretists who rejected semantics altogether in favour of "pure visuality, the text as texture, and the constructivist possibilities of words" (Bayard *New* 21).

aligns the constructivist desire for a non-semantic language, centred on the detachment of signifier from signified, with Foucault's Classical (i.e. Cartesian) episteme, where identity is substituted for the analogies of the earlier episteme. For Foucault, the Classical sign "enables things to become distinct, to preserve themselves within their own identities, to dissociate themselves or bind themselves together" (*Order* 61). By disassociating signifier from signified, the constructivist concretists attempted to provide an autonomous identity for language. Bayard further asserts that both isomorphic and constructivist agendas assume a "primeval ground almost lost beyond recall through the multiplied errors of linguistic figuration" (*New* 37); following Derrida's critique of Western metaphysics, she argues that isomorphic and constructivist concretism are logocentric to the extent that they both posit a "transcendental signified," a meaning that is presumed to be beyond the differential play of language. The isomorphic attempt to equate graphic form with semantic function is based on a utopian desire to fuse objects and signs, to "return" language to an originary space of full and complete presence, as opposed to the absence and difference of representational signification. Henderson claims that the hermetic tradition which Nichol discovered through the Dada sound poet Hugo Ball is based precisely on a desire to return to this sort of divine language, in which the word contains "the essence of the thing itself," instead of merely representing that thing: "Man and God could speak directly, all secrets could be opened" ("Radical" 117). Similarly, the constructivist celebration of non-semantic experience assumes the existence of a universal language, which will be "understood" because of its immediate self-presence. In a 1963 letter to Pierre Garnier, for example, Ian Hamilton Finlay illustrates this typical concretist ideology by claiming that his poems stem from a need to be "embodied in the perfection of absolute, non-thinking life" (84), thereby aligning his version of concrete with the desire for a logocentric ground.[A] American visual poet Karl Kempton similarly continues to draw on the writings of Carl Jung and Robert Graves to claim that visual poetry "may provide clues into the process of merging with the greater mystery" (94).

The TRG demonstrate a similar type of nostalgic desire for full presence in their discussion of geomantic translation:

```
a.i.o.ua.eo.a.u.a     (((((((((((
a.eo.o.ua.eo.a.u.a    ))))))))))
e.a.o.a.ao.o.u.e      ((((((((((
ei.aoe.a.e.oae        )))))))))
```

```
e.ue.eaa.a.e.u        (((((((((((
o.ae.e.o.a.o.ue.a     )))))))))))
a.u.i.ea.ia.a.ae.u    (((((((((((
e.o.a.e.a.oea.o.a.ea  )))))))))))))
a.o.a.ao.o.u.ui.o     (((((((((((
a.aa.a.oa.oi.a.aea    )))))))))))
a.u.i.ai.ea.a.e.o     (((((((((((((
i.a.eaa.a.u.a.a.a     ))))))))))))
a.u.i.o.o.u.o.oa.a    ))((((((((((((
                      (()))))))()
```
*(Rational* 33).

Theoretically, the auditory and rhythmic structures in the left column translate "a linguistically felt energy field of opposing and merging forces," represented by the brackets in the right column (33). The TRG define this energy pattern as a "configuration of discharges (graphic or semantic) arising from a reader's engagement with a text (semantic and phonic recognition, denotations, connotations, intertextual associations, etc.)" *(Rational* 153). Much like the concretist version of the transcendental signifier discussed by Bayard, this procedure reveals an overwhelming desire for a "natural language" of full presence, in which word and object are directly connected. By realigning the linguistic material in the left column into a graphic organization of space in the right column, the poem attempts to remove translation from "an informational service—the one's tongue's access to other tongues" *(Rational* 32), and to institute instead a direct connection between a non-semantic "energy pattern" and a universally comprehensible sign-system. Like the other modes of non-referential translation practised by the TRG,[T] geomantic translation stems from a concern for "the elimination or limitation" of "the post-Babel condition of man that so many mythologies reflect" *(Rational* 32).

## 2. The Politics of Magic

Is the TRG's opposition to this post-Babel condition through geomancy a means to murder the Name of the Father, or is it exactly the reverse: an unconscious support for the transcendental signifier as Fatherly phallus, and the symbolic order which it erects? This question could be set slightly askew by thinking about what is seen and what is not seen in the poem. Seen: the geomantic translation in the column to the right of the reader functions as the "divine" side of the poem, perhaps indicating an unconscious debt to early Christian iconography, where the blessed souls are represented at the right hand of Christ. A series of letters (enroute to their destination in the symbolic) are placed in the left column, with the damned. Unseen: the central place traditionally occupied by the deity in Christian iconography is here represented by a blank space, equivalent to the invisible and non-existent Other, whose gaze evokes the subject's desire to see what is not shown—i.e. the subject's desire to see the Other. For Lacan the gaze is situated outside, where it reveals the mastery of the subject by the Other: "I am looked at, that is to say, I am a picture.... What determines me, at the most profound level, in the visible, is the gaze that is outside" (*Four* 106).[15] As a modality of the Other, the gaze reinforces a social text that is always already in existence by "picturing" the subject, creating the subject in its own image. Given the importance of spatial organization in concrete discourse (including blank and em ty space), this misreading is not as far-fetched as it might seem at first glance. The blank at the centre of the poem exists as an invisible presence which separates and structures the sacred and the profane. In effect, it functions as the type of icon that Lacan considers valuable precisely because: "the god it represents is also looking at it. It is intended to please God. At this level, the artist is operating on the sacrificial plane—he is playing with those things, in this case images, that may arouse the desire of God" (*Four* 113). If we replace the word God with the Name of the Father—a substitution that has its precedents in Lacanian discourse—the blank at the centre of the translation may be read as an unconscious intertext for the desire that the Name of the Father elicits from its subjects. Moreover, the blank space at the heart of the poem is analogous to Lacan's theorization of the anamorphic stain.[16] When it is viewed straight on as an empty place

---

[15]In French, both the Sartrean look and the Lacanian gaze are termed "*le regard.*" In contrast to the Sartrean Look, however, the Lacanian gaze cannot be pinpointed, contained, or returned, and this accounts for its capacity to disturb the subject's imaginary misrecognition of unity, thereby constituting the subject as lack.

[16]Lacan interprets the mis-shapen skull in the foreground of Holbein's painting *The Ambassadors* (1533) as a key example of *anamorphoses*. This object can be seen as a skull only when perceived from a specific angle: "the secret of the picture is given at the moment when, moving slightly away, little by little, to the left, then turning around, we see what the magical floating object signifies. It reflects our own nothingness, in the figure of the death's head" (*Four* 92); "Holbein makes visible for us here something that is simply the subject as

through which "a.i.o.ua.eo.a.u.a" moves to become "((((((((((," it remains without meaning or significance, but when it is seen from a psychoanalytic angle it is recognizable as Other; geomantic translation follows a route through the Other's gaze to arrive at its final destination, which turns out to be none other than the transcendental signifier.

McCaffery's *Carnival The First Panel 1967-70* was published in 1973, the same year as the TRG's report on translation and geomancy. The text's introduction calls for the dismantling of boundaries between form and content, and then links this breakdown to a spiritual goal: "the duality between form and content can no longer be maintained / thus for the modern writer form will have a directly spiritual meaning" (n.p.).[WX] Similarly, in *Carnival The Second Panel 1970-75* (1977) McCaffery writes that the text's roots extend beyond concretism to "labyrinth and mandala, and all related archetypal forms that emphasize the use of the visual qualities in language to defend a sacred centre" (n.p.). These two examples illustrate McCaffery's early desire for the Other as transcendental signified. Paralleling the goal of geomantic theory, the texts attempt to fuse together signified and signifier, visual form and spiritual content. In a 1987 interview with Nichol, however, McCaffery remarked that he now finds the "actual content" of *Carnival* to be embarrassingly naive, although he remains impressed at the "absence of a subject in the two panels" ("Annotated" 72). As Warren Tallman remarks: "given his atheism, Steve does not want the word to be with G_d" (267).

Nichol, on the other hand, remained interested in geomancy and the links among religion, myth, magic, and language throughout his writing career.[Y] His 1985 claim that the "disintegrative tendency in art ... is in fact an attempt to regain the magic" of organic totality ("Passwords" 11) is clearly symptomatic of a nostalgic longing for the Other as a total and unified presence. In "The "Pata of Letter Feet" (1985) he further presents the view that art and magic are connected activities by arguing that the letters of the alphabet are trace memories of Norse runes:

what disappears in the notion of the norse runes is any idea of a signified or referent. i have a mental image of the signifier but the act of writing it down does away with its referential value since i am in the act of invoking the thing itself i.e. literally bringing it forth into the moment of the writing (95).

---

annihilated. . . . the subject in question is not that of reflexive consciousness, but that of desire" (*Four* 88-89).

Nichol's construction of the non-referential rune is based on his recasting of Saussure's binary theory of the sign. He connects language with invocation:

'A' (the signifier) together with 'A' (the mental concept and, therefore the signified) constitute a sign that we agree will trigger the sound 'A'.... This notion of something triggering something else (in this case the eye triggering the tongue & ear, translating an impulse from a visual medium to a sound medium) is, after all, a pretty fair definition of what the power of invocation is supposed to be ("'Pata" 82).

Nichol considers the rune as a type of pre-Babel object that unifies form and content. His continued legitimation of the connection between a spiritual ground and the non-referential signifier is radically different from McCaffery's view that the referent is a linguistic analogue to commodity fetishism.[J] By stressing a pseudo-religious Ur-language, Nichol sidesteps McCaffery's critique of referential writing's capacity to hail subjects as unquestioning consumers.[EE] Nichol's desire for an original language of full presence appears relatively conservative in the light of McCaffery's highly politicized theoretical position.

# An H in the Heart

During a 1982 panel discussion with George Bowering and Daphne Marlatt, Nichol claimed that he would refuse to publish with McClelland and Stewart, because "they think they're going the distance if they give you a choice of two typefaces! They've really busted their hump for you as author—'Hey, this stuff's not going to sell anyway!'" ("Syntax" 35). Nevertheless, in 1994 McClelland and Stewart published a "bpNichol reader" entitled *An H in the Heart*, an easily digestible collection which appears to be modeled on such consumer friendly texts as Viking's *The Portable Faulkner* (1947) and *The Portable Joyce* (1954)—selections which integrate these writers' more easily assimilated texts with short, absorbable extracts taken from their "difficult" writing. The Nichol reader is edited by Bowering and Michael Ondaatje, and includes selections from his poetry, prose, and theoretical writing with the TRG. Bowering writes in the text's introduction that he hopes poetry readers and teachers who are unfamiliar with Nichol's inventions "will find something that might lead them into the labyrinth" of his other writings (xiii), but he forgets to mention Nichol's refusal to publish with a commercial publishing house. On the one hand, the book provides a good introduction to Nichol's writing outside of *The Martyrology*, as well as a potentially valuable pedagogical tool for illustrating the type of reading demanded of much contemporary poetics. Furthermore, the anthology is faithful to Nichol's desire to print in various different typefaces. On the other hand, however, the text's publication by Canada's most highly visible literary press operates against the aesthetic and critical agendas that Nichol helped to create and foster among the Canadian small-press publishing industry.

*An H in the Heart* includes excerpts taken from Nichol's collaborative TRG work—ironically, it also reproduces one of McCaffery's own visual poems, falsely attributed to Nichol. But by removing the TRG reports from the politicized context of *Open Letter*, *Rampike*, or another of the small press journals in which they first appeared, the text downplays the reports' radical challenge to consumer culture. Nichol's and McCaffery's critique of mainstream publishing is evident in several of the TRG collaborations which theorize the links among reading, the book, and commodity culture. It is worth quoting two prominent examples from the TRG reports:

There seems to exist at present a dichotomy in attitude between the book as a machine of reference and the book as a commodity to be acquired, consumed and discarded (*Rational* 62). The book's primary status is that of object; a homogeneous mass-produced item subject to the forces of market economy, the general logic of commodities and the ideological effects of the cultural industry (*Rational* 179-180); 184).

In the M&S collection, however, this sort of conspicuous inquiry into the politics of mass production disappears. The TRG reports seem farcical in the context of *An H in the Heart*. For example, "Reading and Writing: The Toronto Research Game" (1982) employs chance operations and foregrounds the instability of meaning to skew communication, thereby constructing the reading process as a sort of writing, where readers creatively work to produce social meanings. However, unlike the TRG reports mentioned above, the M&S collection elides any overt theoretical statement about the politics of reading. Critical theory in *An H in the Heart* is limited to aesthetic games. Granted *An H in the Heart* is a "bpNichol" reader rather than a collection of TRG writings, but Nichol also expressed concerns about commodity culture apart from his TRG work. In his 1976 interview with Caroline Bayard and Jack David, for example, he claimed that his early writing was "designed to slow down the reader and to force the person into a contemplative mood. It resisted consumerism" (22).

By publishing Nichol in a format that he expressly criticized while alive, McClelland and Stewart detach his writing from the authority of its author. In this respect, *An H in the Heart* supports the now commonplace critical assumption that authors are not the masters of their own discourse. Yet the figurative death of *An H in the Heart*'s author does not only come about as a result of the birth of its reader. Authorial death occurs with the birth of the publisher—i.e. the publisher's *labour*, its ability to give birth to the text—without the presence of a father, but with Bowering and Ondaatje as midwives. Of course, M&S has produced a large number of significant volumes of Canadian poetry, and it would be difficult to argue that poetry is not a marginal form to begin with. Yet because Nichol was so vocal about the publishing industry, the text's refusal to address its own mode of production is problematic.

To his credit, Bowering carefully outlines some of the collective hesitations a group of Nichol readers had about producing the anthology: "Can this bpNichol reader coexist with the books produced with such nice attention by the non-profit presses? We decided that we wanted for Barrie what he never asked for himself—a hefty collection in the mainstream" (xiii). However, this statement reduces Nichol's critique of commodity culture to mere modesty, thereby fostering the idea that Nichol really wanted to publish with a mainstream press all along, despite his frequent statements to the contrary. The term "hefty" further undercuts Nichol's work with minimal forms such as his boxed shuffle text *Still Water*,[C] as well as with ephemeral pamphlets such as his *Absolute Statement for My Mother*.[B]  Frank Davey and Nichol argue in "The Book as A Unit of Composition" (1985) that the "various standard components of a book—its title page, half-title page, colophon, its typeface, columns, margins, gutters, signatures, paper—have the potential to participate as signs within the writing" (40); *An H in the Heart* disregards the importance they place on the book-as-object. The collection closes with a list of some of the small presses in which Nichol was originally published, and encourages readers to "seek out many of the texts as they originally appeared" (235). Ironically, however, the list of sources is headed by a quotation from Nichol: "[little presses] are the only true friend of poetry" (233).

The publication of this book apart from the marginal presses supports the positive critical reception that Nichol's writing has received from within the literary academy. As Jeff Derksen remarks in "Mapping Minds, Mapping Frames: *The Martyrology* and its Social Text" (1998), Nichol's long poem may indeed represent the "outer conceptual horizon of official literature in Canada" due in part to the large body of critical writings that the text has stimulated (51). Derksen argues that the critical reception of *The Martyrology* situates the text:

into a matrix of cultural limitations of Can Lit. At the same time this [critical] writing has perhaps enlarged these limitations, as [Frank] Davey proposes [in *Canadian Literary Power*], adding another conceptual horizon to what can be 'meaningful' or 'readable' within this particular national literature (51).

*An H in the Heart* collects material written apart from *The Martyrology*. Yet the re-positioning of Nichol's work apart from its small-press context illustrates the extent to which his writing has enlarged the conceptual horizon of "official" Canadian literature. In this respect, *An H in the Heart* operates as a material site for the authorization of formally innovative poetics; the text works in tandem with institutionalized critical and pedagogical discourses (such as this book) to produce a Nichol industry.

What ideological effect occurs when Nichol's texts enter a different economy of relations? To what extent does the growing Nichol industry contribute to his writings' domestication? From the beginning of his career, Nichol linked his stress on process and on textual play with social revolution and personal revelation.[A] But because the "bpNichol reader" recontextualizes Nichol's writing within a "hefty collection in the mainstream" (for mainstream, read market-economy) the text tends to normalize and domesticate the incomplete process of that social revolution. *An H in the Heart* offers us a *retro* nostalgia for the glory days of the counter-culture, somewhat analogous to the ideological orientation of the 'classic rock' radio stations now bombarding the airwaves. In both instances, consumers—not all of whom are baby boomers—find idealized dreams of the revolutionary past. Rather than producing a critical re-interpretation of Nichol in the light of our present social situation (as in the case of McCaffery's footnote revisions to the TRG reports collected in *Rational Geomancy*[F]), M&S manufacture a de-politicized product for commercial exchange, thereby producing a text that is not structured around community and the type of equitable social relations that Nichol affirmed in his writing. While it would be naive to suppose that the industries of literary criticism and book publishing could somehow escape the constraints of market economy, the TRG's conspicuous questioning of that economy suggests the need for further critique, at least in relation to the Group's own texts. This capacity to critically self-reflect on cultural production is precisely what is missing from the bpNichol Reader. As Žižek reminds us, social structures will be maintained when their enjoyment is materialized in specific social practices[C]; as long as the Nichol industry neglects to critically consider the material sites of its own production, that production will ensure the continued enjoyment of commodity culture, as well as the particularly unquestioning mode of social relations which that culture constitutes.

# Intertextuality

## 1. Thrust

In "The Search for Non-Narrative Prose" (1975), the TRG consider text as an "axis along which reading and writing exist as non-dialectical terms; a suggestion of both reading and writing as two methods of identical, textual engagement" (*Rational* 134). Opposing the conventional treatment of writing as the active transmission of meaning to a passive reader, the TRG argue that the "referential thrust" of content connects divergent texts together, until "a highly complex inter-textual network evolves with codes established and referring out to more texts which then enter the sphere of actual reading" (134).[D] In effect, they construe text as the site for a dialogic relationship among reader, writer, and a network of texts.

Much like Kristeva's discussion of Bakhtin's theory of intertextual process as the situation of a text "within history and society, which are then seen as texts read by the writer, and into which he inserts himself by rewriting them" (*Desire* 65), the TRG's discussion assumes a heterogeneous and polymorphous body of texts that surround the reader as re-writer. For both Kristeva and the TRG, intertextuality is a dynamic process, where pre-existing texts generate new texts. Kristeva's claim that the "literary word" is "an *intersection of textual surfaces* rather than a *point*" (58) concurs with the TRG's claim that "content will appear as the sum total of referential thrusts" (134), because both theories assert that signifying practices are multiplicities which exist in relation or opposition to other signifying practices. For the TRG, the kinetic movement of intertextuality challenges the notion that textual problems are "static properties" (134); kinetic movement is analogous to Kristeva's intersecting textual surfaces, while static properties are analogous to her literary word as a single point.

## 2. Last Word A

The TRG's early consideration of intertextuality as a writing of reading has informed both Nichol's and McCaffery's own writing procedures.[J] In

'Ow's "Waif" (1975), for example, McCaffery uses prepared "supply-texts" which function as the:

total available language system for the poem—a specific limitation of vocabulary. The supply-texts were chosen at random* from books, articles, magazines, newspapers etc that happened to be close to me at the times i felt the urge to write (n.p.).[17]

Drawing on intertexts as diverse as Newton's *Optics*, Susanna Moodie's *Roughing it in the Bush*, and a trigonometry textbook, McCaffery reconfigures reference, sound pattern, and line length. In "Newton's Optics Two" he writes:

> in a very dark chamber at a round hole about the
> blue and turned and inch broad making the shut
> the blue window where i placed the glass shut
> and the prism whereby turning blue it made shut
> upwards towards the opposite way to turn blue
> as it shut a coloured form it turned blue the
> axis of the prism passing that shut in the glass
> the blue end and the one end in a very dark blue
> was followed shut at the other end (n.p.).

Although the diction of this passage comes from Newton's *Optics*, the poem moves away from the meaning of the supply-text by foregrounding the materiality of the signifier, through the use of repetitive and paratactic patterns of randomly selected words and phrases. The indeterminacy of lines such as "turned an inch broad making the shut / the blue window" challenge pictorial and propositional reference; ironically, McCaffery destabilizes pictorial imagery by re-writing a supply-text which originally focused on light. And since "Newton's Optics Two" is drawn from the writings of one of the most significant founders of modern science, its intertextual re-writing offers a critique of the lucid rationality of scientific discourse, and undermines the tie between light and rationality that gave the Enlightenment its name.

A good example of a less random approach to intertextuality occurs in McCaffery's 1991 poem "Lastworda," published in *Theory of Sediment*.

---

[17]McCaffery uses supply texts on a number of occasions. In *Dr. Sadhu's Muffins* (1974), for example, he writes: "in most cases the word selection for any one poem was determined by a non-intentional reading among a supply text chosen at random from whatever happened to be on or near my desk" (n.p).

Beginning with currently circulating words ("intervention buffer friendly to diskette that transit via chunnel"), the poem's diction and orthography grows increasingly archaic ("pvblique straine in hvmane politie foorth stept obloquie tooke"), until it moves through Middle English ("bokes of gramer to be bowghte") and then concludes with Old English ("hetelic weard fela heahfaestne fleon lastworda"). McCaffery notes that the poem "retreats a few lines to each decade.... Whenever possible I've tracked down a word's *first* appearance in print" (*Theory* 214). The text is both horizontally synchronic ("mvckhinder hvnge the flottin lvmpe") and vertically diachronic ("spandex ... U-boat ... 'tis ... rulynge ... swerode ... cnihtum"). If we were to read this poem through the TRG's claim that content appears as the "sum total of referential thrusts" (*Rational* 134), its content would be the entire English language, situated on a historical continuum, because content here consists not only of the material signifiers that are present in the poem, but also of the intertextual network of metonymically contiguous signifiers which are absent from the poem—i.e., with the various historically shifting versions of Saussurian *langue*. "Lastworda" piles these materially absent but metonymically connected *langues* on top of other *langues* like the sediment of the book's title.

### 2. Local Materials

Louis Zukofsky's *"A"* - "15" (1964) begins with a homophonic transla-tion of the Hebrew book of Job. For Ron Silliman, *"A"* - "15" and Zukofsky's other homophonic translations justify the "primacy of the signifier as the dominant feature of language" (143); however, the poem's intertextual re-writing of Job, passages from Edward Gibbon on barbarism and civilization, references to Odysseus, Nestor, and other figures from Homer, as well as to J.S. Bach, Lucas Cranach and John F. Kennedy, indicate that the text engages with more than signifiers detached from cultural tradition. Along with this social intertextuality, *"A"* also represents Zukofsky's personal life through references to his family and his neighbourhood.[18] As Silliman comments,

---

[18]See Barry Ahearn's *Zukofsky's "A": An Introduction* (1983) for a biographical approach to the poem. For Silliman, Ahearn's integration of *"A"*'s disparate elements in a chronological structure based on Zukofsky's biography problematically humanizes the text and takes the reader's attention away from "what was actually right there on the page" (142-3).

Intertextuality 61

no other practitioner of the American longpoem has so thoroughly located the events of her or his telling in the actions and structures of the poet's own daily life. Yet the process of composition has so transformed these referents into textuality that an opaque music of hollowed-out signifiers is often felt to be the result. (142)

*"A"*'s transformation of personal and social reference "into textuality" make it a significant precursor to *The Martyrology*'s problematic engagement with self and textuality. As we have seen, *The Martyrology*'s later books construct an indeterminate interchange of textuality and bodily experience, thereby potentially dismantling the binary opposition between speech as "body syntax" and writing, while simultaneously re-claiming self presence through the formal deployment of lyric subjectivity.[D N] Silliman's claim that *"A"* never resolves the "equilibrium of the spoken within the written within the spoken..." (128) could equally be applied to Nichol's longpoem. For example, consider *Chain 1* of *Book 5*'s journey through the Annex streets in Toronto. In the line "Wal Mer's pa Dina Madi'[s] son" (n.p.), Nichol reconfigures three streets from his own neighbourhood—Walmer, Spadina, and Madison—by breaking down the street names and recombining them into the characters Wal Mer (who has a pa) and Dina Madi (who has a son). The next stanza, "(her one & / only)

images of / ancient lineages" tells us that the personified street Dina Madi has only one son (suggesting an affinity with Christ and echoing *The Martyrology*'s religious dimension), while further re-introducing the genealogical theme of the earlier books. Of course, the ancient lineages could also refer to the linear grid-system of Toronto streets, thereby further collapsing the difference between textuality and location; Nichol's poem

> A
> LAKE
> A
> LANE
> A
> LINE
> A
> LONE

is now a literal concrete poem, etched in the cement of "bpNichol Lane" behind Coach House Printing, just a few blocks from Walmer, Spadina, and Madison. The passage continues:

> St Orm the saint of ships and seas
> was he Wal Mer's father
> Dina Madi's son
> & if the one
> then all these names could be
> nicknames
> for claimd similur things

This stanza includes several devices which turn our attention away from reference towards the materiality of the signifier, such as the use of paragrams (St Orm/storm)[P]; interlingual translation (sea/Mer)[T]; rhyme (son/one); self-reflexivity (names could be/[bp]nicknames); unconventional spelling (claimd similur). Here Nichol treats his own local environment as a text to be re-written. The poem further continues mapping streets until it reaches "the bluer strait / streets / houses lived in my time," thus constructing an unresolved difference between speech and writing in the near homophones bluer strait and bloor street, along with an autobiographical reference which eventually dismantles itself: "(ideals arrayed against the actual i deals)." Much like Silliman's reading of Zukofsky's *"A"*, *The Martyrology*'s compositional process transforms geographical and autobiographical details into textuality, and textuality into a local site for the voice.

   *The Martyrology* is a "hysterical" text, because its negotiation of reference and non-reference problematizes the seemingly unified logic of the symbolic network. Not hysterical in the Freudian sense of the term (an explanation of bodily symptoms resulting from repressed memories) or in Mary Jacobus' important feminist re-visioning of Freud ("'Femininity' and 'hysteria' name the otherness or strangeness which inhabits psychoanalytic theory (and literature) and which psychoanalysis must marginalize in order to found itself as a theoretical body of knowledge" [200]), but in Žižek's politicized reformulation of the term to indicate the subject's resistance to interpellation:

what is a hysteria if not precisely the effect of a testimony of a failed interpellation; what is the hysterical question if not an articulation of the incapacity of the subject to fulfil the symbolic identification, to assume fully and without restraint the symbolic mandate? (*Sublime* 113).

*The Martyrology* exhibits hysterical symptoms by blocking the subject's desire for the full presence of meaning. While the fundamental experience of the subject is lack because of obstructed desire, Žižek argues that the central experience of the hysteric is the inversion of this obstruction, wherein the hysteric converts blocked desire into the desire to be blocked, or in other words, converts the desire to know into the desire for ignorance (*For* 144). Instead of following a desire for satisfaction, *The Martyrology* desires dissatisfaction through indeterminacy. The text desires to have its desire for meaning impeded, in order to frustrate the misrecognition of symbolic totalization as a ground for interpellation. This is not to say that *The Martyrology*'s various indeterminacies cancel its over-riding tendency towards lyrical subjectivity and self presence, but that the self that is continually displayed in its pages hysterically rehearses its own refusals and acceptances of meaning.

# Jabès, Deconstructive Theology, & the Mystical Referent

In "A Throw of the Dice" (1981), the Group juxtaposes a number of quotations found in Mallarmé, Kafka, Derrida and especially Jabès, whose work they claim was "riveting our attention and constitute[d] the bulk of the quotations" (*Rational* 196). Why this special attention to Jabès? Derrida tells us that Jabès' texts show how both commentary and poetry are forms of exiled speech: "In the beginning is hermeneutics. But the *shared* necessity of exegesis, the interpretive imperative, is interpreted differently by the rabbi and the poet" (*Writing* 67). For the rabbi (and the scholar), the act of interpretation is interpreted as a search for final truth. Interpretation is a road followed in order to find an origin. For the poet, however, the interpretive act is not interpreted as a search for origin or truth, but is instead a means to maintain the play of interpretation. McCaffery and Nichol choose to remain exiled in the interpretation of interpretation as play: "A poet's is not a scholar's research and these [TRG] reports make no pretence to a professional legitimation or an academic's rigour" (*Rational* 12).[M] In other words, the TRG do not conceive of their reports as attempts to describe, decode, or evaluate texts, but as an intertextual site for poetic (re)writing.

Derrida's discussion of the difference between rabbinical and poetic interpretation illustrates his debt to Jewish tradition; unlike the Greco-Christian tradition which has constructed writing as a necessary evil, an instrument which can only imperfectly reveal the *Logos*, Judaism has foregrounded the importance of writing by treating writing itself as sacred. Morny Joy characterizes Derrida's writing as a mirror of the "Jewish estrangement from easy solutions. It is a hermeneutics of exile, of absence, of constant interrogation" (274). This type of estrangement is evident in the TRG text's representation of a single quotation found in Derrida's "Edmond Jabès and the Question of the Book" (trans. 1978):

THE NONQUESTION OF WHICH WE ARE SPEAKING IS THE UNPENE-
TRATED CERTAINTY THAT BEING IS A GRAMMAR: AND THAT THE
WORLD IN ALL ITS PARTS IS A CRYPTOGRAM TO BE CONSTITUTED

OR RECONSTITUTED THROUGH POETIC INSCRIPTION OR DECIPHER-
ING: THAT THE BOOK IS ORIGINAL, THAT EVERYTHING BELONGS TO
THE BOOK BEFORE BEING AND IN ORDER TO COME INTO THE
WORLD: THAT ANYTHING CAN BE BORN ONLY BY APPROACHING
THE BOOK; AND THAT ALWAYS THE IMPASSABLE SHORE OF THE
BOOK IS FIRST (193-194).

The "book" that precedes the world suggests the influence of a Kabbalist-
ic theory of writing on Derrida, for as Harold Bloom notes, "kabbalah
speaks of a writing before writing (Derrida's 'trace'), but also of a speech
before speech" (52). For Joy, Derrida's discussion of Jabès' *Book of
Questions* (1963) suggests that if Derrida believed in a God, "it would
only be in a God whose very existence was a question mark, an enigma,
whose (non)existence echoed through all human deliberations of his
purported signs" (274-5).

Nichol's deconstructive negotiations with religious discourse[N] typically
take on a specifically Christian (rather than Jewish) orientation, even
though that orientation is far from orthodox. Saints derive from Christian
discourse, Martyrologies are Christian texts, *Book 2* of *The Martyrology*
includes a "Book of Common Prayer," and Nichol frequently refers to the
New Testament. The combination of Christian references and deconstruc-
tive poetics in Nichol's longpoem situate it in the apophatic or "negative"
tradition of theology. Negative theology is a (non)discourse by which
knowledge of the divine is achieved through successive denials of the
divine. For Kevin Hart, Derrida's questioning of all systematic knowledge
is structurally analogous to mystical theology; even though Hart acknowl-
edges that Derrida is not a theologian or mystic, and that there may be no
thematic link between deconstruction and mysticism, "there may well be
a structural link, in that mystical theology is a mode of deconstruction"
(45). Hart argues that the negative theologian places theological language
"under erasure" (203), meaning for Hart that s/he uses the language of
theology against itself: the positive theologian makes claims about what
God is, while the negative theologian uses the positive theologian's
vocabulary to describe what God is not. Hart quotes from the writings of
Pseudo-Dionysius to exemplify theological language under erasure:

nor is It personal essence, or eternity, or time; nor can It be grasped by the
understanding, since It is not knowledge or truth; nor is It kingship or wisdom;
nor is It a one, nor is It unity; nor is It Godhead or Goodness; nor is It a Spirit, as
we understand the term, since It is not Sonship or Fatherhood (176).

Pseudo-Dionysius negates terms traditionally applied to God by positive theologians in order to state what God is not. Significantly, the form of his discourse deconstructs the idea that the deity exists as a positive term, such as the Archimedean point of the Greco-Christian *Logos*. This move maintains metaphysics to the extent that it maintains a desire for the deity, while simultaneously deconstructing that desire by foregrounding the deity as différance, as text. This strategy is precisely the approach followed by Nichol: "& God of (the many) (no) names / who is (the one) (the many) / (above) (around) (inside) all / (watched) (did not watch) over everything" (*Book 4, Chain 1*). By negating God's names and actions through contradictory anti-logic, and by upholding the desire for a God who cannot be known through language, Nichol continues the iconoclastic tradition of negative theology.

Charles Taylor remarks that for Jabès "one of the pseudonyms of the Unnameable Other is 'God'" ("Series" xiv). Although Nichol's numerous writings on the sacred concur with the negated form of Jabès' unnameable deity, McCaffery is an atheist who loves the non-referential text—not as an iconoclastic sign for an unrepresentable God, but as a challenge to referential fetishism. True, the religious dimension of Nichol's approach seems incompatible with McCaffery's materialist poetics. Yet these approaches are not entirely polar opposites. Because of their shared desire to problematize representation, McCaffery and Nichol share the same type of *structural* link that Hart finds existing between Derrida and the apophatic theologians. The similarity stops at this structural level, however, because McCaffery regards reference as a political rather than a spiritual issue. His desire to criticize the dependence between capitalist and linguistic structure augments Silliman's claim that the referent is perceived in capitalism as a commodity fetish—an argument built on Marx's contention that capitalist ideology legitimates the relationship between people and commodities over the relationship between people. For Marx, commodities take on the character of "metaphysical subtleties and theological niceties," because they operate as fetishistic sites for the condensation of all social and economic relations between human beings; in a commodity

the social character of men's labour appears to them as an objective character stamped upon the product of that labour ... the relation or the producers to the sum total of their own labour is presented to them as a social relation, existing not between themselves, but between the products of their labour (215-216).

For this reason, the "mystical character" of commodities does not originate in their use-value. Silliman develops this notion by arguing that capitalism produces and consumes reference as a commodity fetish:

Words not only find themselves attached to commodities, they *become* commodities and, as such, take on the 'mystical' and 'mysterious character' Marx identified as the commodity fetish: torn from any tangible connection to their human makers, they appear instead as independent objects active in a universe of similar entities, a universe prior to, and outside, any agency by a perceiving Subject. Thus capitalism passes on its preferred reality through language itself to individual speakers (8).

For Silliman, the disappearance of the poetic word (i.e. the disappearance of tangible qualities such as graphic notation and sound pattern) occurs as a result of the capitalist situation of subjects "into a series of more or less identical units," such as the modern unemployment line or the contemporary mass market novel, where readers can passively consume a story that "appears to unfold miraculously of its own free will" (13). For McCaffery, the referential "strategy of promise and postponement" has roots in religious discourse, because it derives from "an earlier theologicolinguistic confidence trick of 'the other life'" ("Intraview" 189). Yet the "mystical character" of the referential word as commodity fetish differs from the non-word of apophatic theology, because the mystical theologian negates rather than affirms reference. As Hart remarks, the epistemological problem of negative theology is "how to talk properly of God when language can only improperly signify Him" (6). In any case, McCaffery supports Silliman's theory by offering a materialist critique of the referential fetish, which he claims "wants a message as a product to be consumed with as little attention as possible drawn to the words' dialectical engagements" (*North* 152). As such, his writing is a site for social struggle.

# Kristeva / Lacan

## 1. The Phenotextual Book-Machine

The TRG's discussion of the physical properties of the book-machine, entitled "Rational Geomancy: A Realignment of Kinships 2" (1981), is divided into two bands of type: the top is written by Nichol and the bottom by McCaffery. In their introduction to the article, they write that the two bands were intended to "bring into play the dialogic possibilities and properties of the page" (*Rational* 165). While Nichol's band primarily describes various types of unusually produced book objects, and McCaffery's band analyzes rather than describes some of these objects, "numerous cross-overs" occur between the two bands (165). Regarding the lengthy discussion of scratch n' sniff books in the upper band, the lower band questions whether the "tactical recovery of the oral, tactile, and olfactorial traditions" of the book-machine show evidence of the return of a "prelinguistic body, a genotypical corpus, back into writing" (173). Although McCaffery does not mention Kristeva directly in this article, his affirmation of the prelinguistic body and the biological genotype as sites for "writing" is reminiscent of Kristeva's theory of the genotext, especially when we consider McCaffery's frequent citations of Kristeva. Genotext is a Kristevan term for pre-Oedipal drive energies, a generative process which can be detected in:

phonematic devices (such as the accumulation and repetition of phonemes or rhyme) and melodic devices (such as intonation and rhythm), in the way semantic and categorical fields are set out in syntactic and logical features, or in the economy of mimesis (fantasy, the deferment of denotation, narrative, etc.).... even though it can be seen in language, the genotext is not linguistic (in the sense understood by structural or generative linguistics). It is, rather, a *process*, which tends to articulate structures that are ephemeral (unstable, threatened by drive charges, "quanta" rather than "marks") and nonsignifying devices that do not have a double articulation. (*Revolution* 86-7)

For Kristeva, poetic language is revolutionary to the extent that its radically heterogeneous non-signifying activities challenge the unified subject of the symbolic order. This challenge informs the lower band's suspicion about the revolutionary character of the book-machine. Instead of centring on the formal possibilities of the book-machine, as in the upper band ("the book's machine potentials similarly allow the innovation of texture"), the lower band argues that the book's physical properties legitimate conventional reference. The operator of a scratch n' sniff book does not necessarily achieve an unmediated relation to an extra-linguistic referent, since the smells are still "framed rhetorically and enclosed within the presidency of narrative." (174). Because of these anti-revolutionary referential properties, the lower band situates the book-machine in opposition to the genotext, within what Kristeva would label as the *phenotext*—i.e., "language that serves to communicate, which linguistics describes in terms of 'competence' and 'performance'" (*Revolution* 87).

Even though the text is collaborative, the diction and argument of the lower band's analysis clearly owes more to McCaffery than to Nichol. Unlike Nichol, McCaffery offers a critique of how the book-machine is complicit with established modes of commodity fetishism. Ironically, the physical placement of the analytic band of text beneath the descriptive band mimics the topographical relationship between the book-machine and its political unconscious.[B] McCaffery raises Kristeva's theory of the genotext only to illustrate how the book-machine fails to function along the lines assumed by her analogy between poetic language and political revolution.

## 2. Psychoanalytic Genealogy

McCaffery frequently cites the importance of Lacan's theories to his own writing projects. Yet he is far more Kristevan in his approach to writing than he is Lacanian.[EE] In a 1984 interview with Andrew Payne, for example, McCaffery claimed that Lacan best elucidates the radically textual nature of subjectivity, and that we "inhabit and inhibit an unconscious that is structured by a language" (*North* 129). After observing that Lacan's development of Freud puts "the very notion of a subject in doubt and, at best, poses that subject on the ruined concept of a self" (129), McCaffery argues that we would "best look for a viable notion of subject in something like Kristeva's notion of a subject-in-process within an instinctual and symbolic economy" (129). Similarly, in a note to his early article on sound poetry entitled "Lyric's Larynx" (1978), McCaffery argues that psychoanalysis offers an alternative tradition to sound poetry's roots in Dada and Futurism. This other tradition would stress the "Freudian and Lacanian implications in current semiology" (*North* 183). McCaffery does not develop this notion according to Freudian or Lacanian models, however, and suggests instead that Kristeva's theory of a subject split between "bio-physical processes" and "social constraints" can best account for the sound poem as "the textual embodiment and performed manifestation of these subjective determinations of utterance" (184). McCaffery sets up his note on sound poetry by assuming a Lacanian perspective, but then turns to a Kristevan theory of the subject which is radically different from Lacan's theory. For Lacan, the Other which precedes the subject of language is the place of the signifier and the pre-condition of subjectivity as lack. Kristeva, on the other hand, conceives of the Other as a "threshold between two heterogenous realms: the semiotic and the symbolic" (*Revolution* 48). The eruptions of semiotic pulsions within language do not only provide examples of desire and lack, but also of surplus pleasure, of a "jouissance that divests the object [the signifier] and turns back toward the autoerotic body" (49). Differing from Lacan's totalizing theory of subjectivity as lack under the Other's all-seeing gaze, Kristeva's theory of the split subject challenges the homogeneous dominance of the Other.

### 3. Motherhood According to Steve McCaffery

In *Textual Politics and the Language Poets* (1989), George Hartley constructs a convincing analysis of the link between minimalist art and McCaffery's writing. Minimalism blossomed during the 1960s and early 70s, and was based on: "direct perception of objects, which in painting are the lines, colours, forms, and not on symbolic interpretation of them, as when a line is used to express a subjective emotional state of the artist" (Leepa qtd. in Hartley 81). The work of minimalist sculptors such as Donald Judd and Carl Andre stemmed from a phenomenological concern with subject and object; in order to emphasize the interaction of the object, gallery space, and viewer's perception, the typical minimalist sculpture was pared down to a bare minimum of surface detail. Minimalist objects were intended to force viewers into an awareness of their own bodies, as objects in space in relation to other bodies. For Hartley, minimalism offered some poets a way to question the role of frames in constituting experiences (81). He writes:

Just as in sculpture where the gallery room is seen as a field in which presences sit in a spatial relation to each other and to the shape of the room itself, negative space thus signifying as much as the objects within it—so the page of the minimal poem here is to be seen as a field in which graphematic presences sit in various relationships to one another (83).

Hartley points out that McCaffery's reduction of the sign to a "cipher" foregrounds the role of syntactical frames in the creation of meaning, thereby making the reader more conscious of the framing process itself. McCaffery provides an example of the cipher in "The Death of the Subject" (1977):

```
            al(t    ch
    ph      ysto            kl
                ee
       apl
    sta
            )
                ry (63).
```

Much like the objects of minimalist sculpture, the cipher operates as an "emptied sign ... a sign removed from function ... to be observed and experienced as event per se" ("Death" 64), as well as *the sign for attention itself* (75). However, McCaffery further proposes that readers either "encipher" the text as a complete and immediate surface event, and/or "decipher" the text for its potential to expand toward "semantic normality" (64). For Hartley, these gestures toward interpretation transform the minimalist concern with the rejection of meaning into a positive concern with the basic elements necessary for meaning. On the one hand the cipher provokes a minimalist negation of meaning in favour of the viewer/reader's phenomenological experience of space, while on the other hand it provokes the possibility of reconstructing semantic normality. The cipher's double orientation thus makes Hartley critical of McCaffery's construction of "an ambiguous fusion of both negative and positive impulses" (82).

By reading Language writing in general as a productive challenge to Capitalist ideology, Hartley claims that it questions "not just what we think but also the way we structure what we think" (98). But he finds the ambiguity of the cipher problematic. Hartley is upset by the genotextual contradiction of the cipher, and neglects Kristevan semiotic productivity for a phenotextual argument, from which he frames the poetry inside the theme of a questioning of frames (his approach is understandable, given the conventions of the academic genre he employs—i.e., the legitimation of understanding and rigour *qua* knowledge). Nevertheless, the cipher's ambiguity operates precisely as a semiotic disruption of the type of phenotextual order assumed by Hartley's critique. McCaffery does not cite

Kristeva in his discussion of the cipher, preferring instead to refer to examples drawn from the writing of contemporary North American poetry. Yet the aporia he constructs in the cipher is certainly consistent with the mode of productivity that Kristeva asserts is integral to the semiotic/symbolic interchange. This productivity is especially evident in relation to the influence of visual art: as a non-discourse working in tandem with the symbolic to produce the subject-as-process, the semiotic is not pictorially representable in conventional symbolic terms, but appears whenever form breaks away from theme, implying that semiotic eruption is the "real, objectless goal" of a visual image (Kristeva *Desire* 248). For McCaffery, the reader/viewer is caught in a liminal space between the "literate and the perceptible," and the particled form of the cipher is "fragment only if the mind cares to retreat back into its familiar lexical associations and refuse to take a stand upon the dialectical pinion of the seen and the read" ("Death" 75). We could of course apply a Lacanian critique to this liminal state, by arguing that McCaffery's distinction between the seen and the read is a misrecognition, and that the Other's gaze evokes lack and desire in both visual and verbal registers. But if we focus instead on the Kristevan subject, it becomes evident that the contradiction of McCaffery's double orientation is far more sympathetic to Kristevan productivity, than it is to the largely pessimistic Lacanian subject of lack in the Other. By short-circuiting the difference between seeing and reading, McCaffery sets up a semiotic gap, thereby calling the unicity of the symbolic order into question. When McCaffery asserts that the cipher is a "strategic method of creating non-commodital process-products" (67), as well as a "paraverbal surface on to which the reader is invited to step into productive effort" (71), he assumes the type of poetic revolution—as a metaphor for the disruption of social and linguistic order—that Kristeva proclaims in her early writings on poetic language.

# Manifesto

In their 1973 Manifesto, the TRG assert that "all research is symbiotic & cannot exist separate from writing" (23). Symbiosis is the association of two different organisms, usually two plants, which "live attached to each other ... [and which] contribute to each other's support" (OED). By constructing a symbiotic relationship between research and writing, the TRG propose that research is an ongoing process, occurring in and through the writing itself rather than before the fact of writing. McCaffery in the introduction to *Rational Geomancy* writes that a "poet's is not a scholar's research and these reports make no pretence to a professional legitimation or an academic rigour" (12);[1] unlike scholarly research, which attempts to describe, interpret, and evaluate precisely a text or the relationships among texts, the TRG research assumes an intertextual and (re)productive engagement with outdated forms. As Scott Pound points out, the TRG's research is "the inverse to the institutionalized application of theory" (1). Linda Hutcheon's *The Canadian Postmodern* (1988) provides an example of institutionalized theory; Loraine Weir argues that Hutcheon normalizes politically radical texts by "domesticating deviance and inscribing it within her postmodern paradigm" (181). Similarly, Alan R. Knight's "The Toronto Research Group Reports: A Myth of Textuality" (1985) domesticates the reports by downplaying their various contradictions: "at the early stage in the discussion of these reports, it is more worthwhile to discover a myth, which means to discover, or create, a sense of coherence" (102). Although Knight argues that the TRG deconstruct the "myth" of objective criticism in order to replace it with a new "myth of textuality" based on issues drawn from French theory, the heterogeneous character of their project makes any construction of a unified master narrative on their writing highly questionable, and his article thus rehearses the type of problem that Weir finds in Hutcheon.

Associating theory with a "reflective practice that assumes a prescriptive and appropriative stance before the object of its field,"

McCaffery describes the TRG's research as "annotated booklists, *catalogues raisonées* of a described, analyzed, and frequently little-known texts [sic], juxtaposed upon a cultural grid we both considered to be paratactic" (*Rational* 12-3). In other words, the objects of their research are texts which they recycle in order to create new texts, within a new social context. The traditional scholar constructs an authoritative monologue, whereas the TRG constructs a dialogic response—in Nichol's words, "an articulation of a particular (to this writer) understanding ... which may offer a way in for others if they choose to take it" ("Contributed" 13). Nichol's statement on research is similar to his often quoted[19] 1967 statement on poetics: "I place myself there, with them, whoever they are, wherever they are, who seek to reach themselves and the other through the poem by as many exits and entrances as possible" (*Journeying* n.p). Neither McCaffery nor Nichol consider writing to be the formal container for research as content, but blur the border between the two activities, and invite readers to enter into their dialogue.

In "Growing Hegemonies: Preparing the Ground for Official Anthologies of Canadian Poetry" (1990), Knight argues that prefaces to English Canadian poetry since the 19th century have attempted to impose unity on Canadian writing, thereby constructing a Canadian tradition. For Knight, the metaphor of organic unity employed in these prefaces valorizes similarity rather than difference. Opposed to discontinuous, indeterminate, or incoherent forms, the organic metaphor: "as model of wholeness can be applied not only to the exegesis of single texts but also to anthologies prefaced as if they were single texts, since these prefaces attempt to integrate the greatest number of textual elements" (Knight 146). Unlike the prefaces criticized by Knight, the TRG reports do not uphold a Canadian tradition. However, by proposing to create an organic partnership between research and writing, the TRG's manifesto *prefaces* their later reports with a unifying model. True, these later reports are often formally heterogeneous, and they often focus on radically different forms.[20] Yet the manifesto's emphasis on organic symbiosis seems to

---

[19]The quotation is the epigraph to Roy Miki's *Tracing the Paths* (1988) and Sharon Thesen's *The New Long Poem Anthology* (1991).

[20]The different forms of TRG reports include not only discursive prose, but also a design for a board game ("Reading & Writing: The Toronto Research Game"), a *fumeti* ("Nary-A-Tiff"), and notes for performances. Their subject

undercut difference in favour of homogeneity. This contradiction prompts the question: when is symbiosis not symbiotic? E.D. Blodgett criticizes the use of organic metaphors in Canadian prefaces because they tend to "obscure the constructed character of any literary discourse" (xiii). If we read the manifesto through Blodgett's critique, the symbiotic metaphor employed by the TRG naturalizes the link between research and writing, because symbiosis assumes a natural, as opposed to a constructed, attachment between organisms. Yet organic symbiosis is not the only position presented by the TRG manifesto. Earlier in the text, the manifesto asserts that action is different from writing, but that research is still a form of action: "where action eliminates the need for writing research can function to discover new uses for potentially outdated forms and techniques" (23). If we were to read this statement literally, and not to conceive of the word "action" as a synecdoche for political actions such as labour strikes, demonstrations, or the reader's productive role in the creation of meaning,[BH] we might find that the text offers us a significant contradiction: if research is action, and action is not writing, then research cannot be writing. The manifesto's construction of a symbiotic attachment between writing and research contradicts their construction of a difference between writing and research. The point here is that this seemingly marginal contradiction actually foreshadows the multidirectional and unregulated drift of the future reports. The manifesto's call for symbiosis is in effect one element in what Deleuze and Guattari would term a rhizomatic system; unlike the limited organic connection between trees and their roots: "the rhizome connects any point to any other point, and its traits are not necessarily linked to traits of the same nature; it brings into play very different regimes of signs, and even nonsign states. The rhizome is reducible neither to the One nor the multiple" (*Thousand* 21).[B] The TRG manifesto is irreducible to the organic unity of its own rhetoric, since symbiosis is not the only structure it upholds. Organic unity operates as yet another of the many interconnected systems within the TRG multiplicity.

Perhaps this multi-directionality is a rhetorical gesture, intended as a playfully ironic equivocation and designed to amuse the readers of *Open*

---

matter ranges from Children's books to Renaissance poetry to comic books to contemporary theory: "[i]ntertextual travels that cover Husserl, *Reader's Digest*, Robert Filliou and Maurice Sendak are as valid as those covering Max Brand, Stan Lee, Jacques Lacan, T.S. Eliot and Robert Crumb" (*Rational* 156).

*Letter.* In "Violence and Precision: The Manifesto as Art Form" (1984), Perloff argues that the Dada manifestos of Tristan Tzara are often indistinguishable from prose poems, because of their complex network of concrete but ambivalent images, and elaborate structures. Perloff concludes that unlike Italian Futurist manifestos, which were intended to move the masses to action, Dada manifestos were intended to "charm and give pleasure to one's coterie, to those who are like-minded" (92). Given the TRG's large debt to Dada,[c] it is certainly not inconceivable that the ironic paradoxes of their manifesto follow a similar program.

For the TRG, "all manifestos are simply statements of progressive awareness" (23). Because this assertion constructs manifestos as provisional statements of changing awareness, it appears to be against any construction of a totalized and completed position. However, the adjective "all" restricts the scope of manifestos: could we not construct a post-liberal, post-1970s manifesto which stated a politically *regressive* awareness, such as a neo-con manifesto? This legitimation of progressive awareness reveals a remnant of enlightenment discourse in the TRG's writing, for the manifesto shares with the enlightenment the belief that the individual and society progress through indistinct ideas toward an awareness of knowledge. The cultural logic of enlightenment discourse is progress.

And yet, the TRG progress toward a discourse which de-legitimates the notion of progress. Reading the manifesto as one term in a line of descent which includes their later citations of Barthes, Derrida, Kristeva, and other French poststructuralists—writers who de-centre the logic of the progressively enlightened individual, and assume the death of the subject of rationalism—we can fully appreciate Foucault's claim that genealogy refuses to demonstrate the active existence of the past in the present. To cite just one of many examples, the Group's 1973 call for a rationally progressive awareness is remarkably different from their 1982 de-centring of the subject in language: "all the world's a page and all the men and women merely signifiers" (*Rational* 227). For Foucault, genealogy identifies "the complete reversals—the errors, the false appraisals, and the faulty calculations that gave birth to those things that continue to exist and have value for us" ("Nietzsche" 146). The TRG begin their journey in an ideology that legitimates rational awareness, and arrive at an ideology that calls into question the subject of that awareness. Paradoxically, they reach their later position only when they move through an ideological space that is completely at odds with their destination's ideology. The false consciousness of rational individualism, expressed in the manifesto, gives birth to the death of the subject of rationalism in the later reports. This is not to say that there is no similarity between the manifesto and the later reports, since (as I argue above) the manifesto's assumption of an alternative role for readers is consistent with the TRG's later critique of commodity culture. This genealogy makes evident a significant tension within the TRG's discursive formation—i.e., their reversal from an unstated but undeniable acceptance of rationalist progress, toward a suspicion of the rationalist project of progressive knowledge. Tension arises because this reversal paradoxically comes about through the acquisition of a mode of (theoretical) knowledge that casts doubt on the veracity of knowledge itself. Perhaps the generic conventions of the manifesto call for the type of totalizing narrative assumed by the subject of rationalism; if so, it is no surprise that the TRG do not publish another manifesto.

# Notation

*1. The Prosody of Open Verse*
Nichol's and Davey's "The Prosody of Open Verse" (1984) details various forms of notation with examples drawn from Canadian poetry. They claim that the contemporary line "is not necessarily a simple graphing of the poet's speech pattern but can be a deliberate enforcing of primary stresses to create particular content and/or rhythmic effect" (359), and they further downplay the importance of speech in favour of the way that notational elements such as the use of line breaks, multiple margins, embedding (i.e. intertextuality), and punctuation produce and control meaning. Ironically however, one of the prime examples of the importance of orality in "The Prosody of Open Verse" concerns Nichol's notation of speech: "bpNichol removes the silent letters from words like 'thought' ('thot') or 'through ('thru'). The effect of such variant spellings is to emphasize the poet's concern for the oral dimension of the poem" (364). Nichol returns to his concern with speech in his 1985 interview with George Bowering and Daphne Marlatt: "when you're trying to notate your breath, what you're going to get is the syntax of your body" ("Syntax" 32).[D] This individualistic body-syntax implies that Nichol's notation is a specific and controlled response to his own material body.

*Book 5* of *The Martyrology* is structured by a series of chains of thought, image, and event; these chains are notated in the text as footnotes that represent reading choices. Readers can either read through the text from front to back, or can choose to diverge and follow one of the various numbered chains. In *Chain 1*, for example, one can follow the pun on Toronto Street names, "'Brun's wick ken'dal[l]'[3]" with the passage:

> set ablaze by light
> it was the light!
> a candle
>         (Kendal)

burning

    hierarchies suggested in a reading ...

or one can follow the path indicated by the superscript number [3] that follows the word "ken'dal[l]" and move to *Chain 3*:

    frag/
      /ments re
    /turn

    /complete
    the sense ...

Notice how the direction of the slash marks ("/") descends from the upper right to the lower left, a formal device that visually mirrors and completes the sense of the linguistic text by physically notating a re-turn to the left margin. Even though the two passages are written in a typically open verse form, in which the exact notation of space on the page "scores" a physical body, the chains ensure that no two readings will follow the same sequence. Once a reader enters the labyrinth of *Book 5*, the number of potential sequences, re-readings of fragments of the same passage, and combinations of different passages, expand as the chains begin to overlap and circulate through one another. On one hand, the text upholds speech through the precise notation of bodily presence, while on the other hand its multiple reading chains foreground writing and difference.

In "'Making in a universe of making' in *The Martyrology*" (1988) Shirley Neuman remarks that "the process of Nichol's notation is his only truth, his only beauty, all he can know in this world" (67). For Neuman, wordplay pluralizes the sacred: "in a parallel to the frequent play in *The Martyrology* on *word* as "w or d," the Lord becomes plural, "l or d." (66-67). Neuman considers Nichol's illustrations of the imprecision of language, through the precise notation of paragrams[P] and puns, as moments of epiphany, with the exception that unlike the epiphanies of Modernism Nichol's epiphanies are "always produced through the letter or the word *qua* letter or word, never through image or symbol" (67). The type of epiphany described by Neuman is applicable to *Book 5*, because the text's notational system—its double disposition between speech and writing—pluralizes the logos. While it is true that *The Martyrology*'s tendency towards lyric subjectivity does not entirely disrupt the self-present unity of the logos, the text's hostility to conventional representational practices (such as the use of images or symbols) indicates a desire for non-mediated communication with a divine Other.[AG]

Nichol's approach to the divine word is remarkably similar to Kristeva's discussion of the French 17th-century mystic Jeanne Guyon in *Tales of Love* (trans. 1987). Guyon's writings construct the self as "an unnamable nothingness, without sight or thought, and yet glorious in the knowledge that it is within the Other's love" (302); the opposition between speech and writing in *Book 5* similarly means that subjectivity is formally enacted as being lost at the surface of language, even though that subjectivity finds itself unified enough to narrate its own loss. Nichol's self-present representation of an absent self further engenders an affective celebration of "every(all at(toge(forever)ther) once)thing" (*Book 5, Chain 10*). Kristeva's words on Guyon could equally be applied to *The Martyrology*:

Perhaps a possibility of stretching the borders of the nameable beyond the boundaries set by a discourse of methods and ideas: by transposing into signs not so much the experience of a subject as fulcrum of reason, white washed analogue of the creating God, as that of a loving subject, an array of constant presences and absences, a dialectics of losses and fullnesses (312-313).

Split between the loss of presence and the fullness of absence, *The Martyrology* both maintains and expands the methodological boundaries of open verse notation as set out by Davey and Nichol. Questioning the logos as guarantor of origins and unified subjectivity, this dialectic further implies a reader as subject in process, split between biology (speech and the body) and the symbolic order.

## 2. Rears its Ugly Head

We could alternately draw on Lacan's ideas to think of the reader of *Book 5* as a model of the subject of lack, trapped in a never-ending circuit of linguistic absences. *Book 5* behaves as a *mise en abyme* of the Other, for it mirrors on a small scale the dialectical condition of the subject in language: supporting the reader's free choice, the text upholds the subject's misrecognition of self as author of its own discourse, and its chains reduplicate the signifying chain of unfinalizable meaning. Nichol clearly desires to be read not according to this Lacanian approach, but through a more productive model, for *Book 5* follows what the TRG describe as "non-narrative writing," which they define as:

writing which ceases to be a re-creation of the writer's creation and becomes a creative product by the reader from elements pre-selected by the writer. . . . Meaningful movement depends (in non-narrative writing) on the reader's productive role in reading. The writer does not predetermine his work's sequence but rather leaves the act of sequencing to the reader. The writer simply delimits the choices (*Rational* 112-113).

The TRG claim that non-narrative writing invites the reader into a dialogue, because it abandons speech as its only model, in favour of the "pure object or play" of textual dialogue between writer and reader. Yet the textuality of the letter does not remove it from the signifying chain and the dialectic of desire in the Other.[A] Nichol's assumption of freely chosen reading paths neglects to account for the theory that all choices remain textual, and hence are stimulated by a desire for consumption.

### 3. The Libidinal Martyrology

McCaffery's writing apart from the TRG also upholds this dialogic conception of readership, yet he dispenses with the type of notational control assumed by Nichol. In his 1974 "Note on the Method of Composition" for instance, he writes "the less care and responsibility i took with any formal matters the more complex and absorbing were the poems that resulted" (*Dr.* 137). Frequently relying on source texts and predetermined chance procedures for the arrangement of material, McCaffery's form offers a critique of speech:

... retina detached a single eye is open subject to the violence of a vacant gaze throughout the length it reaches down into a form of products squares quadrilles each fragment passing down thrown out deluded by itself one eye closed barefoot in a formulas desire displaced the feign to be a wedge a you by ruse a character whose character must end refracted ... (*Black* 148).

This passage, taken from McCaffery's "An Effect of Cellophane" (1989), is not formally constructed according to the type of governing pause discussed by Davey and Nichol in "The Prosody of Open Verse" and upheld by Nichol in "Syntax Equals the Body Structure," although its lack of terminals and punctuation still control reading by posing text as uninterrupted flow. McCaffery instead foregrounds writing as text, detached from speech. There is no place in the text for a speaking reader to catch his or her breath; as D.M. Owen writes, the text is "a writing that could be breathed by no one" (29). "An Effect of Cellophane" exhibits several recurring patterns of imagery, such as the thematics of vision ("retina" "eye" "gaze" "refracted") and division ("detached" "fragment" "displaced" "wedge"). These repeated patterns are reminiscent of some of the characteristics of open verse writing,[21] yet the text's lack of terminal pauses marks a diminution of the value given to breath and presence by Nichol in "Syntax Equals the Body Structure."

Unlike *The Martyrology*'s deconstruction of the speech/writing binary, McCaffery's text inverts the speech/writing pair, thereby re-inscribing a hierarchical structure in reverse. However, given the gaps of referential meaning in "An Effect Of Cellophane," this inversion maintains the type of libidinal economy that McCaffery calls for in his theoretical writings.[E] [K/L] The unresolved tension in this poem is not between speech and writing, as it is in *The Martyrology*, but between the symbolic order and semiotic disruption, a tension that is marked through indeterminate meaning and logical discontinuity. Notwithstanding McCaffery's suggestion that *The Martyrology*'s fundamental indecisiveness may be regarded as irresponsible, and that its lack of overt investigation into the politics of form may be considered ideologically conservative ("In" 80, 86), both *The Martyrology* and "An Effect of Cellophane" problematize the humanist subject of knowledge, the subject who can respond to the question "who is speaking?" with the word "I." Nichol maintains this "I" through the employment of a lyric voice while simultaneously turning to notation to situate that voice between absence and presence. McCaffery differs from Nichol by abandoning the formal notation of a speaking and breathing "I" altogether, in favour of a breathless writing, entirely detached from a speaking voice as unified guarantor of self-presence.

---

[21]For example, Robert Duncan's conception of rime, which Davey summarizes as "the measurable distance between two corresponding elements, whether they be phonetic units, stress patterns, images, or whatever" (298).

# $O$rgans

## 1. Selected Organs

Aside from the few references to the body that are scattered throughout the Group's collaborative reports, their research does not tend to concentrate on the relationship between writing and the body. This is not the case in their individually-authored texts. For example, Nichol's *Selected Organs: Parts of an Autobiography* (1988) is an autobiography written "through anecdotes which had their origin in the various parts of the body" (n.p.). The text's 10 chapters (on the vagina, mouth, tonsils, chest, lungs ["a draft"], fingers, hips, anus, toes, and finally, a sum of the parts) are presented in a style "borrowed from the oral story-telling methods" of Nichol's grandmother. In the "Vagina" chapter which opens the text, he writes:

Doorway. Frame. Mouth. Opening. Passage. The trick is to get from there to here through her. Or the way Ellie misread that sign on the highway for years: RIGHT LANE MUST EXIST. And of course its the old conundrum—the exit's the entrance. Exit Ma & I exist. And when I fell in love with Ellie I was entranced. Into a world. The world. This world. Our world. Worlds (11).

This passage brackets two sets of five short chi(org)asmic sentences: doorway/worlds; frame/our world; mouth/this world; opening/the world; passage/into a world. Conflating the erotic and the maternal, Nichol represents the vagina as both an entrance and an exit, a threshold where the inner folds open to fill-full a bracketed absence. The text's concern with birth continues in the "Mouth" chapter by depicting baby bp's acquisition of language: "I shouted waaa when I was born, maaa when I could name her" (15). The distinction between shouting and naming, between "waaa" and "maaa," is equivalent to the distinction between speech and writing, because the non-word "waaa" assumes a pre-linguistic subject, while the word "maaa" assumes a symbolic text in which the subject is positioned in language. However, the dialogue between the bodily source of speech and the social, abstract paradigm of writing is here represented solely in writing, rather than through the material notation of bodily process, as it is in *The Martyrology*.[DN]

*Selected Organs* disrupts the generic conventions of autobiography to the extent that it represents the organs of a particular body, rather than a sequence of life events. In "The Fingers," Nichol writes:

one day one of his hands turned to him and said: 'Hey, bp, what do you think?' And it had always been his fingers talking, his fingers shaping the letters, the words, that funny grip around the pen, the language, and he lifted his hands up, opening and closing his fingers, and said: 'Nothing' (37).

This passage values the importance of the material body for writing while downplaying the significance of thought. Yet its regard for the body at the expense of thought does not occur formally through the type of physical notation that is present in the open-verse model. Unlike *The Martyrology*'s notational body as process, split between speech and writing, the textual body in *Selected Organs* remains exiled in writing.

Nevertheless, this exiled body is not as logocentric as it might seem at first touch. Nichol's body is segmented and laid out in selected chapters which deal with the individual body parts one by one. His text's organizational structure anatomically dissects the body into a measurable group of components, thus seeming to mirror the rationalism and order of scientific discourse. Foucault argues in *The Order of Things* that difference, measurement and enumeration inform the "classical episteme" of post sixteenth-century Western culture; the sign in the classical episteme allows "things to become distinct, to preserve themselves within their own identities, to dissociate themselves or bind themselves together" (*Order* 61). Nichol's text appears to be consistent with this discursive formation, because it selects and analyzes different organs, thereby establishing them as particularities that stand apart from one another, and which order the world: "the bpNichol liver, the bpNichol kidney, the bladder, pancreas, b p - collected workings I think of as me" (*Selected* 52). However, the text's narration of the tactile and smelly juices of the material body destabilizes the type of visually distinct metaphors which have so often been associated with Rationalism.[22] In "Fingers" for example, Nichol concentrates on touch: "He was not to finger himself (which made his fingers

---

[22]See Martin Jay's *Downcast Eyes: The Denigration of Vision in Twentieth-Century French Thought* (1993) for a survey of the critical turn from the representation of visual metaphors.

stickey), or her (which made his fingers stickey), or stick his finger in his nose (which made his fingers stickey)" (34). Nichol's (hand)ling of the verb "stick" and the adjective "stickey" point to the materiality of the body. Similarly, in "Anus," Nichol further represents smell: "he dropped a rose that smelled like green cheese" (45). The text celebrates the underside of the body through the use of slang ("dropped a rose") and olfactory simile ("smelled like green cheese"), thereby opposing the rationalist affirmation of a dualistic hierarchy which seeks to elevate mind over body. *Selected Organs* thus may be situated in a carnivalesque genealogy that would include Rabelais (as read by Bakhtin) and Bataille, whose article "The Big Toe" (1929) examines the elevation of the head at the expense of the foot ("mud and darkness being the *principles* of evil as light and space are the *principles* of good: with their feet in mud but their heads more or less in light, men obstinately imagine a tide that will permanently elevate them" [*Visions* 20]). The text de-legitimates metaphysics through its representation of a carnivalesque body: "there was a christian recruiting group singing hymns across the street & this car drove by with this guy's ass stuck out the window hanging a moon for the world to see & the choir kept on singing just a closer walk with thee" (44). Nichol's rhyming of the word "see" with the word "thee" aligns visual perception with the Christian deity, thereby seeming to uphold the traditional privileging of sight over touch or smell. Yet this rhyme is carnivalesque to the extent that it ironically undercuts the metaphysical character of "thee" by unifying it with a school-boy prank; in words borrowed from Bakhtin, the text constructs "on that space where the destroyed picture of the world had been—a new picture" (177).

## 2. Random Organs

In *Panopticon* (1984) McCaffery writes through the double disposition between semantic loss and gain that he calls for in his critical essays, where he constructs the loss of semantic meaning as an analog to the affective discharges of a biological body. Any attempt to describe the plot of *Panopticon* would reduce it beyond recognition. As Rafael Barreto-Rivera writes, the "story, which never entirely unfolds ... gives the superficial impression of not being essential to the work. It is ... merely the excuse for the *écriture* that evolves, the subject of which really is, of course, the writing of the book itself" (41). *Panopticon* enacts a baroque circling back on its own language, recontextualizing signifiers in multiple combinations, thereby foregrounding the production and expenditure of meaning. The text refers to a book entitled the "*The Mind of Pauline*

*Brain*," in which a character reads a book called "*Panopticon*," and watches a film entitled "*The Mark*." The character reads in a review in the morning paper that "*The Mark*" is based on a book entitled "*Summer Alibi*," in which a character reads a book called "*Totallitas*." "*The Mark*," however, is not only the title of a film, but also the title of a book, just as "*Summer Alibi*" and "*The Mind of Pauline Brain*" are both the titles of books and of films. Moreover, *Panopticon* also refers to a book called "*Panopticon*." The text does not order these various texts as distinct and separate entities, or place them inside each other like coherent Chinese boxes, but moves through and among them, thereby destabilizing their referentiality and problematizing the way in which meaning is textually constructed. *Panopticon*'s various perspectives challenge the dominance of a panoptic, unified, and central viewpoint.

For Bernstein, the text's title has an "ominous ring," because the panopticon is an image of surveillance and control (*Poetics* 63). Yet McCaffery's text ironically confronts the panoptic gaze by replacing centrality with margins, the eye of the One with a network of rhizomatic multiplicities. About a third of the way into the text (if one reads it conventionally from front cover to back cover), a page is physically glued on top of another page, allowing most of the under page to show through as unreadable text. A small portion of the underpage is legible, and this portion reveals that the underpage is identical to another page that is glued into the book on top of a blank page, about two thirds of the way into the text. Perhaps "identical" is an inadequate word for the description of this underpage, because although both the underpage and its alternate appearance as overpage consist of the same signifiers, these signifiers are erased when the page first appears, leaving only their trace.[B] In psycho-analytic terms, these multiple erasures and traces of pages under pages may be juxtaposed against Derrida's writing on Freud's "A Note Upon the 'Mystic Writing Pad'" (1924). Freud models the operation of unconscious memory on a child's toy, called the "Mystic Pad," which consists of a transparent sheet of celluloid covering a tablet of wax. A stylus produces marks on the celluloid, but if the transparent sheet is pulled up, the marks are erased, although they leave a faint trace on the wax. For Freud, memory operates analogously to the Pad because it retains traces from past impressions and experiences, even though these impressions may not have been consciously perceived. In "Freud and the Scene of Writing" (trans. 1978) Derrida points to Freud's frequent uses of writing as a metaphor for the unconscious. The Pad is similar to writing because both transcribe differential traces, as opposed to the logos of originary presence. For Derrida, the Pad's operation as construed by Freud suggests that "there is no purity of the living present—such is the theme, formidable indeed for the history of metaphysics, that Freud invites us to pursue" (*Writing* 212). Similarly, *Panopticon*'s multiple erasures and overlaps affirm a meaning which is not a representation of a living present or unified gaze. *Panopticon* inscribes a signified that is always reconstituted by deferral. And unlike the image of a centrally controlling gaze which Foucault uses (after Bentham) to illustrate surveillance and control, *Panopticon* ironically stages the gaze as something that is unable to be located in a single place, as an Other that can neither be found nor returned.

McCaffery's critique of unified perspective is further expressed in the text through his labyrinthine use of shifting and indeterminate narrative focalizers. On the surface of an overpage—which at another place in the text is an underpage of traces—a narrator describes a woman who is commanded by another narrator, in "Chapter Twenty Seven of a book entitled *Panopticon*" to stop reading a book entitled "*The Mind of Pauline Brain*," which the first narrator describes as:

noteworthy less for its verbal content than for the superb illustrations it contains. Seventy nine anatomical dissections. The figure printed on plate one shows the skeletal form of a young woman holding a torn muscle and set against a classical background of architectural caprizzos. The figure is so designed that other figures composed of various parts may be glued over the bare bones. What is left for observation in the cavity of the skull is to be seen in those figures that the woman is currently perusing, those figures designated to form the base of a manikin containing the male generative organs by superimposed figures from plates 57-64 (n.p.).

These superimposed illustrations are absent from *Panopticon*, as well as from the various superimposed texts within *Panopticon*, although the text contains several other anatomical drawings. McCaffery concentrates on the body as the textual instance of an absent signified, rather than as the representation of individual organs as transparent signifiers of an actual body. Following the description of absent figures, a narrating voice of indeterminate identity describes a room, where "beside the book [presumably '*The Mind of Pauline Brain*'], is a small flask of glue, a pair of scissors, and a rule" (n.p.). However, this description is immediately followed by another type of rule: "a rule expressly forbidding further description. The narrative voice is replaced by a small portable cassette tape recorder" (n.p.). The sliding and indeterminate narratives within narratives of *Panopticon* denigrate the particularized and measurable body (the "rule") of scientific discourse. And by problematizing the depiction of a substantial body through the use of unstable narrative frames, McCaffery challenges the living present of a body (as subject); *Panopticon*'s maze-like representations of representations of an already textual body transgress referential stability, and construct the body as a rhizomatic multiplicity of interconnected differences.

# P aragram

In "*The Martyrology* as Paragram," (1985), McCaffery borrows the notion of the "paragram" from Leon Roudiez to discuss Nichol's wordplay.[23] Disarticulating the stable relationship between signifier and signified through its concentration on multivalent language devices such as puns and the foregrounding of individual letters within words, the paragram points to the inevitable "condition of words existing within words" (*North* 65). Nichol's saints, for example, are paragrammatic (eg. st. and/stand; st. rike/strike; st. ranglehold/stranglehold), because they employ identical letters in the same order, but reorganize these letters through the use of spacing and punctuation to produce different meanings. McCaffery draws on Lacanian theory to argue that the wordplay of *The Martyrology* illuminates the indeterminate multivalency of language:

> For Lacan, the unconscious has decidedly paragrammatic resonances, being *structured as a language* which is not at the disposition of its user, but rather erupts through fissures in conscious discourse.... This post-Freudian model of the unconscious (linguisticized and de-natured as it is) opens a model for writing as a lettered production which *The Martyrology* employs to the full (66-7).

While McCaffery builds on Lacanian theory, he neglects Lacan's assertion that the signifier produces desire for what is absent, and centres instead on how *The Martyrology* illuminates radically "'other' meanings within the semantic economy" (67). This "other" is not considered by McCaffery as a site for lack, a theory which is of course central to Lacan. Instead, he reads the paragram as a celebration of eruptions in language which are

---

[23]McCaffery cites a brief note in Kristeva's *Revolution in Poetic Language* on Roudiez's "Twelve Points from Tel Quel" (1974): "A text is paragrammatic ... 'to the extent that its organization of words (and their denotations), grammar, and syntax is challenged by the infinite probabilities provided by letters or phonemes combining to form networks of significations not accessible through conventional reading habits'" (Roudiez qtd. in Kristeva 256).

closer to Kristevan productivity than to the dialectic of desire engendered by the Lacanian Other.[K/L]

For Kristeva, the paragrammatic word is a semiotic "device" which disrupts the linearity of the signifying chain (*Revolution* 152). Paragrams operate as one of several modes that articulate the semiotic chora, a concept that Kristeva describes as being "always already caught in the web of signification... [although] not caught in the same way as the two-sided units of the Saussurian sign" ("Within" 36). Paul De Man notes that Saussure was disturbed early in his career by the notion that Latin poetry may have been structured by the coded dispersal of underlying words or names—a dispersal (or dissemination) that undoes cognition and replaces it with "the uncontrollable power of the letter as inscription" ("Hypogram" 37). Saussure first termed this distribution of the verbal unit an "anagram," but then stated a preference for the term "'paragram"—a term that De Man observes "implies no restriction in the space over which the key word is dispersed. Elsewhere he stated his preference for 'hypogram' (sub-text or, better, infra-text)" ("Hypogram" 37). De Man further remarks that Saussure abandoned his investigation of paragrams by the time he began to deliver the lectures which led to his *Course in General Linguistics* (1916). McCaffery points out in "In Tens/tion: Dialoguing with bp" (1987) that the "non-rational proliferation of meanings" suggested by the paragram "drove Saussure crazy" (73). For McCaffery the paragram "rescues" the sign,

from its definition by Saussure, to gain reconsideration as a complex group of elements in which the letter-sound is granted an 'executive' status, empowered with narrative possibilities (beneath the level of the law of the word) and the ability to generate vast chains of differentials (74).

McCaffery implies that shifting the focus from the word to the letter does not remove the paragram from the signifying chain, and thus his theory does not dispense with the sign altogether, but recasts the paragram in the role of signifier, with multivalent possibilities for meaning in the role of the signified. Against the *Course in General Linguistics*' construction of an arbitrary but unified link between the signifier and its signified (S/s), McCaffery proposes an expansive relation between the paragrammatic signifier and a large number of co-existing signifieds (S/sss...). His construction of the paragram as a means to disrupt syntax, logic and the "closure of an aggregate intention" (*North* 66) affirms difference as a positive term, through which readers might affectively celebrate their own split subjectivity:

We are not far, at this point, from the system of the unconscious, for the implication of the paragram (i.e. meaning's emergence out of a different meaning both of which share common graphic or acoustic components) is that a unitary point of fixed meaning can no longer operate as a binding agent of closure (*North* 69).[24]

McCaffery uses the paragram's openness to create an alternative genealogy for *The Martyrology* stemming from European theory rather than from specifically North American traditions such as Projective Verse and seriality.

Kristeva further theorizes the paragram as heterogeneous and potentially contradictory, as well as politically subversive, because it challenges the ideology of paternal law, built on the differentiation of objects and categories. For Lacan this paternal logic occurs in a primordial form at the mirror stage, and then intensifies with the subject's acquisition of language and subsequent constitution as lack. Contrary to this Lacanian law of the father as the "always already there of language" (*Tales* 44), Kristeva theorizes that the acquisition of language constitutes the subject according to an heterogenous interchange of symbolic and semiotic elements. Even though Kristeva acknowledges that meaning for Lacan is never totalizable, "it is nevertheless *homogeneous* with the realm of signification" ("Within" 35). Kelly Oliver comments that in Kristeva's account Lacan's theory of language "prevents what is heterogenous to meaning—the semiotic—from entering signification" (*Reading* 39). McCaffery's writing on the paragram similarly implies a break with Lacanian theory; just as Kristeva's semiotic disrupts the unicity of the symbolic, McCaffery's theory of the paragram celebrates "the erupt

---

[24]See David Clark's "Monstrous Reading: *The Martyrology* After De Man" (1990) for a further elaboration of the relationship between Saussure's discomfort with paragrams and *The Martyrology*. For Clark, Nichol is similar to early Saussure because both treat texts as if they were "hypogrammatic or paragrammatic, that is, indeterminately bound with several competing signifying strands" (9). Clark further claims that although *The Martyrology* bears trace structures of undecidability, Nichol (like Saussure) ultimately flees the "labyrinthine prospect of a truly infinitized free-play that is irreducible to and unregulated by any system of signification" (13). Unlike Clark, however, McCaffery celebrates the paragram by aligning it with political revolution, a type of recuperation which De Man would likely regard as an imposition on the radical sense-lessness and "uncontrollable power of the letter as inscription."

emergence of plurality through ruptures in the transmissions of the poem's semantic order" (*North* 69).

McCaffery's elision of lack in favour of the "subverted and subverting world" (*North* 69) of paragrammatic discourse appears to present an ideological challenge to the name of the father. However, McCaffery's refusal to follow the implications of the Lacanian theory that he raises might appear as an imaginary misrecognition. Because he downplays desire and foregrounds linguistic rupture as an "expenditure out of semantic's ideal structure into the disseminatory material of the signifier" (*North* 64), his theory could be construed as consistent with the political unconscious of late capitalism, which Jameson problematically theorizes as being marked by fragmentation and the loss of memory; the paragram's particled words and indeterminacy of meaning follow a similar logic. In "Postmodernism and Consumer Society" (1983) Jameson links Language writing with Lacan's conception of schizophrenia, which Jameson claims "emerges from the failure of the infant to accede fully into the realm of speech and language" (118). This failure further means that the schizophrenic is unable to experience temporality: "because language has a past and a future ... we can have what seems to us a concrete or lived experience of time" (119). For Jameson, the formal features of the mass media express this sort of schizophrenic forgetfulness:

Think only of the media exhaustion of the news: of how Nixon and, even more so, Kennedy are figures from a now distant past [this situation has not altered significantly from the early 80s, when Jameson wrote this article; one could say the same thing about the Gulf war]. One is tempted to say that the very function of the news media is to relegate such recent historical experiences as rapidly as possible to the past. The informational function of the media would thus be to help us forget, to serve as the very agents and mechanisms for our historical amnesia" (125).

Jameson argues that Language writing's discontinuities similarly fragment time into a "series of perpetual presents" (125), thereby reproducing and reinforcing the de-historicized amnesia of multinational capitalism. But Jameson's reduction of Language writing to a disease of consumer culture is flawed in several ways. First, it neglects to consider the writing's capacity to provide a critical framework for the investigation of ideology in language. This framework functions more as a diagnoses that as a disease. Second, his critique neglects Language writing's critically collective projects, including such collaborative pieces as *LEGEND*

$(1980)^{25}$ and the network of small-press magazines such as $L=A=N=G=U=A=G=E$ in which poets collectively addressed each other's work. These collective projects significantly redefine established modes of literary production, which in the North American context have traditionally tended to valorize the writer as a heroic individual. Moreover, Jameson omits the collaborative effort that Language writing assumes for its reader. These criticisms might provisionally answer Jameson's concluding question about "whether there is also a way in which it [i.e. "postmodern" fragmentation] resists that logic" (125). McCaffery's work constructs linguistic heterogeneity as process and as a metaphor for social revolution, thereby calling into question Jameson's compression of Language writing to a support for late Capitalism.

---

$^{25}LEGEND$ is co-authored by McCaffery, Bruce Andrews, Charles Bernstein, Ray Di Palma, and Ron Silliman.

# Quarrel

In the TRG *fumeti* (photo comic) "Nary-A-Tiff" (1982) McCaffery kills Nichol, and then thinks to himself "AT LAST I CAN GET SOME SERIOUS WRITING DONE!" (*Rational* 222). The *fumeti* humorously illuminates several distinct differences between Nichol and McCaffery in a highly condensed and farcical form, and these differences further shed some light on the critical reception of their work.

"Narry-a-Tiff" begins in the "PALATIAL OFFICES OF THE TORONTO RESEARCH GROUP," where Nichol criticizes McCaffery for justifying "MORAL WEAKNESS AS 'EXCESS'" (212). Nichol's desire for a moral standard opposes the "FLOURISH OF THE WHIP" (212) desired by McCaffery; the same sort of challenge to conventional morals occurs in McCaffery's writings on general economy and his "interest in the flip side of orthodox value (absence, loss, waste, expenditure, dying)" ("annotated" 82). Differing from McCaffery's love of excessive absence, Nichol desires a transcendental figure (the "father" and "Lord" of *The Martyrology*) who negotiates with but ultimately upholds the inverse of McCaffery's critique of conventional morality: presence, community, conservation, life. McCaffery finds this type of humanistic ideology problematic when he suggests that *The Martyrology* is politically conservative ("In" 86).[N] Yet McCaffery's challenge to orthodox morality stems from his Marxist critique of class culture, and is therefore not to be taken merely as a nihilistic rejection of all morals and concerns for community. Where Nichol hopes for revolutionary change in the light of the logic of spiritual presence, McCaffery considers a materialist revolution that denies the subject's attachment to the logos as a foundation for rational consciousness.

Nichol claims in "Narry-A-Tiff" that McCaffery merely plagiarizes French theory. In some respects, this playful accusation seems to anticipate Bruce Serafin's deadly serious critique of *North of Intention*, although the two approaches are in fact based on completely different assumptions. Serafin constructs McCaffery's writing as:

*colonial*—as work anxious to mimic a body of 'master texts' originating elsewhere.... the true object of McCaffery's attention isn't the indigenous avant-garde, but the great mass of European masters in whose shadow he and his colleagues huddle. The writers that matter in this book are European. They include Roland Barthes, Roman Jakobson, Julia Kristeva, Gilles Deleuze, Ferdinand de Saussure ... (21, 23).

Serafin assumes that the Canadian avant-garde is isolated from the international context of contemporary writing, and criticizes McCaffery for adopting a colonialist mentality.[26] [C] Yet his own anti-theory stance is intimately colonial; by writing that readers will "become unfree" (23) if they rely too much on books as opposed to their own experience, Serafin presents values which resemble Terry Eagleton's description of English literature at the height of colonialism: "English was an upstart, amateurish affair as academic subjects went ... since every English gentleman read his own literature in his spare time anyway, what was the point of subjecting it to systematic study?" (29). Serafin further criticizes McCaffery for forsaking "his native speech rhythms, and in general the bumptiousness of North American English" (23) in favour of a stylistic pastiche of European theory (even though McCaffery comes from Yorkshire). However his dislike of the serious style and tone of theoretical discourse differs from Nichol's dislike of McCaffery's use of jargon. Responding to Jack David's question in *Out-Posts / Avant-Posts* about the TRG's assertion that content is the "sum total of referential thrusts," Nichol claims: "that's a McCaffery-ism. It's really quite simple; I don't know why

---

[26]McCaffery responds to Serafin's article in "Critical Responsibilities" (1990) by accusing Serafin of xenophobia and by suggesting that he "has truly *not* read the book on which he's commenting... the weight of statistical evidence against his erroneous claims renders his accusations without foundation. In a book of 226 pages there are but 26 references to Derrida, 13 to Lacan, and 10 each to Kristeva and Barthes. This hardly seems convincing evidence of a mind co-opted by European ideas. Mr. Serafin's hallucinatory and inflammatory constructs would be laughable if they were not so insulting in their insubstantial pretensions" (24, 25). See also Christian Bök's "Steve McCaffery and his Critical 'Paradoxy'" (1992) for a discussion of McCaffery's response to Serafin. Bök argues that the authoritative stance adopted by McCaffery is parodic of Serafin: "McCaffery criticizes the critical style of Serafin by deploying the critical style of Serafin" (97). Bök further argues that this parodic response puts McCaffery at the risk of having his own intentions misinterpreted.

Steve insists on these ten dollar words" (26).[27][1] Serafin sees McCaffery's language as being derivative of the European "masters" and therefore complicit with colonialism, whereas Nichol criticizes McCaffery for being an intellectual snob.

The climax of the argument occurs shortly after Nichol accuses McCaffery of plagiarism. In a panel  reminiscent of a scene from a shlocky B-movie, McCaffery responds to this accusation by stabbing Nichol in the heart with a letter opener, exclaiming: "I'M SICK OF BEING SNEERED AT! YOU THINK YOU'RE THE ONLY ONE WITH THE INTERNATIONAL REPUTATION?! ... STICK THIS IN GOD DAMN BOOK  29 OF THE MARTYROLOGY! (*Rational* 216; Fig. 5).  Charles Bernstein has written that humorous texts  can mock what we hold most dear, "so that in our laughter we may come to terms with what we cling to" (33). What does  the laughter stimulated by "Narry-A-Tiff"'s textual murder tell us about the criteria for critical evaluation in Canada? While Nichol's writing has been reproduced in several important Canadian anthologies published since the 1970s, McCaffery's anti-humanist stance has  been excluded from these anthologies. For examples, Nichol's  writing appears  in Gary Geddes' *20th Century Poetry and Poetics* (1973); Michael Ondaatje's *The Long Poem Anthology* (1979); Jack David's and Robert Lecker's *Canadian Poetry* Vol.2 (1982); George Bowering's *The Contemporary Canadian Poem Anthology* (1983); and Sharon Thesen's *The New Long Poem Anthology* (1991). None of these  important texts include work by McCaffery. His poetics counters the values and expectations of Canadian commentators and anthologists far more radically than  what Nichol called a "new humanism ... A desire to clarify the soul  & heart" (*Journeying* n.p.). And if, as Davey argues,[H] Nichol's writing  adds another conceptual horizon to what can be 'meaningful' or 'readable'

---

[27]Nichol defines "referential thrusts": "in any text you build up a lot of different references, a lot of signifieds where this word refers to that, that word refers to this. So that this lamp and this candle that we have sitting here on my right become then the sum total of those thrusts or what happens in that crossover becomes the content and that's what I'm writing about. So, in essence, the sum total of everything I refer to is the content. In a way, the talking about it opens up your thinking so that you can look at the text more abstractly which is why Steve tends to put it in what would be regarded as a more scientific language" (Bayard *Out* 26).

Fig. 5. Steve McCaffery and bpNichol. From "Narry-a-Tiff: Written by &
Starring the Toronto Research Group." 1982.

within this particular national literature, McCaffery's writing falls over the

edge of that horizon—over the border, so to speak. So it comes as no
surprise that McCaffery has gained attention from American critics such
as Perloff, Bernstein and Hartley (among others), critics who have
produced significant studies of the international tradition within which
they situate his work. In contrast, Nichol's work has received almost no
critical attention outside of Canada. Where Nichol's work may stand for
the outer limit of meaning and readability in Canadian literature—a limit
that negotiates with some of the more radical notions of subjectivity in
language arising from (and paralleling) contemporary theory, but
ultimately remaining enmeshed in a humanistic framework—McCaffery's
work questions Canadian literary values by presenting a politicized
investigation of the production and expenditure of meaning, within the
broader social context of inter-subjective relations.

# Reading

## 1. Provisional Understanding

Jane Gallop's "The Dream of a Dead Author" in *Reading Lacan* (1985) focuses on Lacan's 1960 paper "The Subversion of the Subject and the Dialectic of Desire in the Freudian Unconscious," in which Lacan discusses a dream quoted by Freud about a dead father who does not know that he is dead. For Lacan the father in the Freudian dream is the Name of the Father, a phrase that represents the symbolic order, the wider social fabric within which the subject exists—in Lacan's phrase—"from the dawn of history" (*Ecrits* 67). So when Gallop writes that Freud's dead Oedipal father "protects the father," she means that the Freudian institution protects the Symbolic Order. The psychoanalyst's claim that s/he can interpret and know, and therefore master, reinforces the hierarchical structure of the Name of the Father. Gallop points out that in the Lacanian paradigm knowledge does not reside in the analyst, or in the analyst's capacity to interpret. Instead, Lacan criticized American ego-psychology during the 1950s for attempting to cover "over the duality of the one who suffers and the one who heals, with the opposition between the one who knows and the one who does not" (qtd. in Gallop 29). American ego psychology:

> theorized that the analyst's "strong" ego would serve as a model for rebuilding the "weak" ego of the patient. Thus the analyst was authorized by his theory to believe in and act out the transferential *illusion*, becoming the good, strong parent, the ultimate role model, without ever questioning the imaginary structuring of that role, nor how it minoritized the patient and enhanced the analyst's self-deluded prestige (29).

According to Gallop this re-evaluation of psychoanalysis has repercussions for hermeneutics, for it calls into question the interpretive powers of analyst and critic.

Although Gallop focuses on the application of psychoanalysis to literature, in which the psychoanalytic critic is endowed with the same illusory power as the psychoanalyst, her critique of authoritative discourse parallels the TRG's critique of the interpreter as the subject presumed to know, in favour of a dialogic relationship among reader, writer and text:

> what we're aiming for ... is a process of questioning which, by its very self consciousness, initiates a process of questioning in *you*—as far as we see it that's your part of this conversation, that's the point at which we feel that we're including you and feel included by you (*Rational* 151-52).

By upholding this dialogic process of questioning, the TRG attempt to dismantle the critic's hierarchical position of power. Instead of writing criticism "which presumes to know more than the writer of the text, taking for oneself the role of the superior & benignly indulgent uncle," Nichol proposes to articulate "a particular (to this writer) understanding" (*Rational* 13). And instead of knowledge, the TRG offer a provisional understanding "which may offer a way in for others" (13). Significantly, the TRG's critical approach attempts to orient interpretation by resituating the occurrence of meaning between the reader and the text, rather than in the text itself, which they do not consider as a stable entity.

## 2. *Affective Transference*

We can further develop the TRG's assertion that any departure from traditional narrative presentation necessitates "a radical psychological change in the reading experience" (*Rational* 82) through Gallop's theorization of the relationship among reading, transference, and desire. As we have seen, the TRG construct reading as a dialogue between text and reader, in which the reader is initiated into a self conscious process of questioning. This process may be regarded in the light of Gallop's claim that reading is something like psychoanalytic transference—i.e., the analysand's act of displacing the introjected figures or objects acquired during his or her life onto the analyst. Transference is the process whereby a patient shifts affect applicable to another person—usually a parent—onto the analyst. By refusing to respond to the patient's expectations during analysis, the analyst creates a type of second, mini-neurosis, in which the analysand behaves toward the analyst as if s/he were father, mother, brother, etc. (this behaviour is labelled the "transference-neurosis"). Theoretically, this second neurosis makes unconscious patterns become conscious to the analysand, thereby allowing unconscious material to be worked through. Gallop claims that the act of reading is similar to the analytic situation, because the reader's introjected internal objects are transferred onto the text (instead of the analyst) in a manner that parallels the transference-neurosis.

If, as Gallop suggests, the reading process is something like a transference, the reader's hopes for knowledge correspond to the analysand's attempt to learn about its own desires—i.e, to learn what those desires are. For Gallop, the unconscious material that is transferred on to the text is desire itself. She writes:

> the desire to know what the Other knows, so as to know what one desires so as to satisfy that desire, is the drive behind all quests for knowledge .... We read to learn what the other (what the Author) knows, to learn what are his desires, in the hope of understanding and satisfying our own (185).

Reading as transference allows us to reconsider the TRG's methods of narrative presentation as a site for readers to recognize their own desire, because the indeterminacies, gaps, and contradictions of McCaffery's and Nichol's writing confirm the applicability of the sort of non-authoritative, transferential interpretive strategy suggested by Gallop. In fact, McCaffery argues that Language writing invites the reader to "step into productive effort" and to read as a "logotherapist" ("Death" 65, 71). Traditionally, the psychological therapist stands in the same relation to the patient as the writer does to the reader, because patients and readers conventionally consider therapists and writers to be subjects presumed to know. McCaffery's construction of the reader as therapist, however, follows the same type of inversion suggested by Gallop. By overturning the typical power relation between analyst and analysand, therapist and patient, or writer and reader, Gallop and McCaffery point to the reader's power to interpret his/her own meanings. Texts such as McCaffery's *The Black Debt*[EE] or *Book 5* of Nichol's *The Martyrology*[N] refuse to provide readers with the illusion of fully present knowledge—an illusion which, when read alongside of Lacan, would seem to bolster up a false sense of unified subjectivity. McCaffery's and Nichol's texts thus function in a similar manner to Lacan's injunction to his own students: "let everybody tell me, in his own way, his idea of what I am driving at" (qtd. in Felman 83-4).

# Sound

In *The New Poetics in Canada and Quebec* Bayard surveys the importance of European sound poets of the 1950s and 60s on the development of Canadian sound poetry. She points out that some sound poems modify existing words, while others are entirely non-semantic, following the type of concrete non-referentiality upheld by Pierre Garnier.[28] Henri Chopin, for example, presented vocal sounds divested of reference, and focused on poetry as a medium "capable of animating human bodies, allowing them to open up to their own biological, physical capacities" (*New* 28).

---

[28]The two categories of sound poetry are similar to visual poetry's split between isomorphism (the fusion of meaning and visual design) and constructivism (in Bayard's sense of the term—i.e. the rejection of semantics altogether). Nichol alternated between both semantic and non-semantic modes of sound poetry, and his aural modification of words led to the same sort of indeterminacy found in the paragram (paraphone?); Sean O'Huigin writes that he played Nichol's *Motherlove* (1968) album to a group of inner city school children in Toronto, and that the children where entranced: "immediately they began to see concrete meanings which even bp had not realized. in his 'mmmmmmmmiiiiiiiiilllllllkkkkk' poem they could visualize a cow, a pail filling up and hear the sound of milk splashing" (212). The children's interpretation illustrates the potential multivalency of the sound text, because they interpret the poem as a representation of dairy farming rather than as a cry for the nourishment from the mother, as the title of the album suggests. Paul Dutton observes that it is impossible to quote in print from sound poems: "you've got to be on the right platform at the time his [McCaffery's] train passes through or rely on secondary retrieval by tape" ("McCaffery" 19). But the problem with recordings is that they de-contextualize the listener's immediate relationship with the performer(s), and vice versa. For Scobie, recorded sound poetry is unsatisfactory because it is removed from "essentially live, often improvised, performances" (*bpNichol* 56). Nichol prefers to avoid the tape recorder because of his concern for the "relation between me as reader and the people who come to hear me. Through sound I could affect them" (Bayard "bpNichol" 33).

This non-semantic branch influenced McCaffery's early theoretical writings on sound poetry. In the introduction to *Sound Poetry: A Catalogue* (1978), he writes that Chopin "makes the decisive break from a phonetic basis to sound poetry.... Chopin's work can be regarded in the tradition of lexical decomposition" (11). He further aligns non-semantic sound poetry with Kristeva's semiotic order: "Julia Kristeva has written of literary practice as being 'the exploration and discovery of the possibilities of language as an activity which frees man from given linguistic networks'.... [sound poetry] takes its place in the larger struggle against all preconditioning" (18). Kristeva's ideas offer McCaffery a means to theorize the potentially revolutionary challenge of sound poetry, in both its historical and contemporary forms. The form as explicated by McCaffery desires a new world which cannot yet be thought or spoken in conventionally semantic terms, except inasmuch as this new world differs from the present social condition. When McCaffery asserts that sound poetry stands against all forms of preconditioning, he frames the genre as a politically radical challenge to established modes of thought. In this respect, sound poetry follows the structural analogy that Kristeva draws between poetic language and political challenge; the sound poem disrupts grammatical and syntactic logic in the same way that revolution disrupts political order.

Scobie comments that Nichol's experience at the Therafields therapeutic community formed the basis of his sound poetry with the Four Horsemen, because the group improvised in "an absolute trust and awareness of each other" (*bpNichol* 19). Therafields borrowed procedures and ideas from William Reich, Arthur Janov, yoga, massage, hypnotism, and a host of other therapeutic practices. The community attempted to bring about the "liberation of the child" within an alternate social context "where adult love and community are possible" (Hindley-Smith 12-13). Nichol worked as a Therafields "lay-analyst" from 1966-1982; McCaffery, Paul Dutton, and Rafael Baretto-Rivera all invested time there during the 70s. However, Scobie's claim that Therafields informed the Horsemen's sound poetry is problematic for two reasons. First, in a 1998 interview, McCaffery asserts that Scobie's comments are "fanciful and perhaps sentimental. The workshops and practices were the sites of tremendous labour and disagreement; there were extreme differences in personality and opinions" (89). Secondly, McCaffery further reports that he remembers "no discussions that linked sound poetry ... to the bio-energetics, psychodramas, and abreactive methods practiced at Therafields" (89). While McCaffery denies that the performances themselves enacted Therafields therapy, Davey points out in a personal correspondence that the aesthetic form of several Horsemen sound poems replicates some of the formal characteristics of therapeutic practice. The performances were not therapy *per se*, even though a remarkable formal similarity exists between the types of non-semantic sounds voiced by the Horsemen and such Therafields techniques as the use of associational word games and primal scream therapy.[29]

McCaffery suggested in an unpublished lecture given at the Poetry Project in New York in 1985 that sound poetry had perhaps "managed to inadvertently privilege lexical meaning by so perfectly exempting it" (qtd. in Coffey 31). His shift away from the form may be due to his growing interest in Bataille; a complete exemption of lexical meaning is restrictive, and thus foreign to the double disposition between production and expenditure that he calls for in his later writing. He first regarded sound poetry as a revolutionary challenge to *all* preconditioning, and later as an inadequate means to provoke social change. More recently, he has characterized the sound work that he collectively practiced during the 1970s and 80s as being both a "poetry of spontaneous affect predicated on a paradigm of unrepeatability" and an attempt to "reformulate the 'poem' as a manifestation of unpremeditated and ephemeral community" ("Voice" 169). This latter stress on the affective nature of the form, coupled as it is with an inquiry into the social relations of a particular community, continues his early work on sound poetry's capacity to question sociolinguistic relations. His linking of affect and community through form illustrates how a specific aesthetic practice can function as the material site for the enjoyment of a sub-culture, a site through which that culture both defines itself as a group, and though which it further unconsciously organizes its own collective affect. As such, sound poetry materializes an ideology by grounding social identity in non-discursive vocalization.

---

[29]Arthur Janov describes the primal scream as "a specific and necessary therapeutic event at certain stages of development, both in life and in therapy. To even try to discuss an early, preverbal trauma (as happens in so many therapies) means to be taken *out* of the feeling and into something countertherapeutic, away from the possibility of final resolution. In this sense we can understand that at certain stages in Primal Therapy the scream *is* curative; it *is* the connection of the early hurt and it is the only possible expression appropriate to the brain at the time of the trauma" (108).

# Translation: *The Martyrology*

## 1. Body Translation

If we no longer consider translation as being necessarily an information service—the one's tongue's access into other tongues—then it can become a creative endeavour in its own right (*Rational* 32).

Numerous examples of self-referential translation occur throughout *The Martyrology*, such as in *Book 6 Books*, where "INK o it / !*whirl*!" functions as a "translation" of "ink eau / ate world." While the oral phonemes remain nearly consistent in both examples, the written text is radically different; aside from the interlingual translation of "o" into "eau," the puns are types of "homolinguistic" translation, where words in the same language sound similar to each other but signify differently when written. Translation in Nichol's writing is both visual and aural, and stems from his experiments with concrete and sound poetry, forms that play with the physicality of language itself. By writing "never easy with these mono themes / mono theisms" in *The Martyrology Book 3*, Nichol translates the first line into the second line—at the level of material signifiers, but not at the level of semantic correspondences between signifieds.

Roman Jakobson's "On Linguistic Aspects of Translation" (1959) categorizes three distinct types of translation: "intralingual translation" (an interpretation of linguistic signs by other signs in the same language); "interlingual translation" (an interpretation of linguistic signs by another language—i.e "translation proper") and "intersemiotic translation" (an interpretation of linguistic signs by non-linguistic sign systems, such as the translation of verbal language into painted image). In *After Babel: Aspects of Language and Translation* (1975), George Steiner observes that Jakobson's third category underlines the notion that a translation is also a transmutation and an interpretation of different semiotic practices. The TRG list Steiner's text in *Rational Geomancy*'s "catalogue of the Group's jointly discussed readings from 1972 to 1984," although they replace Jakobson's "intralingual translation" with the term "homolinguist-ic translation," and "interlingual translation" with the term "hetero-linguistic translation" in the research reports. Steiner writes:

Because it is interpretation, translation extends far beyond the verbal medium. Being in effect a model of understanding and of the entire potential of statement, an analysis of translation will include such forms as the plotting of a graph, the 'making' or 'arguing out' of propositions through dance, the musical setting of a text, or even the mood and meaning in music *per se*" (275).

Jakobson's intersemiotic translation provides a useful means to situate language in relation to the body as a sign system, and his theory could be productively augmented in light of Michael Holquist's discussion of *chronobiology*. In "Bakhtin and the Body" (1984), Holquist writes:

time, long a central category in the speculations of philosophers and the research of physicists, has now become a major preoccupation of biologists ... body clocks organize the activities of cells, tissues, and hormones in a way that uses time to provide internal information about external conditions: the body, in other words, is dialogic (25).

If the body is a sign system, it is potentially translatable.[30] Significantly, the intersemiotic translation of a body into the material condition of writing does not support biological essentialism, because for Bakhtin the external, social context for writing exists in an unfinalizable dialogue with the body.

As we have seen in regard to Nichol's use and theorization of open verse notation, the graphic organization of space on the page represents time: the larger the space, the longer the silence between words.[D N] In effect, spatial notation can be read as a type of intersemiotic translation between the body and language. In "Inchoate Road" from *Book 6 Books*, for example, the word "ocean" is repeatedly rhymed with the word "notion, spelled "*n'ocean*":

    ocean
        n'ocean 'n

---

[30]Pamela Banting uses the term "translation poetics" to signify the writing of a "body back into semiosis, from which it has been exiled from dualist, metaphysical philosophies and theories of representation" (228). Although Banting does not discuss Nichol or Bakhtin, her theory provides a significant pre-text for this section.

```
ocean
        n'ocean 'n
              ocean
                    n' ocean 'n
                          ocean
```

Foregrounding a chronobiological body as text through its intersemiotic translation of internal body rhythms and the external marks of writing, this passage's notation mark it as the site of an intertextual weaving of somatic and symbolic registers.

The many intersemiotic translations of this sort that occur throughout *The Martyrology* serve to emphasize the materiality of both language and bodily experience, and to illustrate the significance of the text's physical surface for its inscription of subjectivity. Nichol claimed in a 1987 interview with Flavio Multineddo:

we tend to use the term 'surface,' certainly in English, almost like a derogatory term; he's very 'surfacy' means 'he doesn't live very deeply in his emotions.' What i'm saying is that right at the surface of the page is where its all happening. What we think of as 'depth in language' nonetheless is just happening because of the stuff right here [points at the page]: all right there on the surface" (15).

The promise of Nichol's translation between material surfaces points to the unfinalized intertextuality of subjectivity, because the interaction of body language and literary language inscribes a subject as text in process. However, the intersemiotic translation of body events does not necessarily imply the presence of a universal, ahistorical, and acultural body language; dialogic relations exist between the body in translation and the symbolic order, because the body is a sign system which cannot exist apart from social phenomena. *The Martyrology*'s implication of a chronobiological body in language invites its readers to apprehend a shared experience of the differential relation between somatic language and the symbolic order, and the text inscribes a subject who is conscious of its body as one of the "linguistic" elements by which it is constituted as a subject.

## 2. Theological Translation

Given *The Martyrology*'s theological orientation, it would not be inappropriate to think of translation in its religious sense. To translate is "to remove the body or relics of a saint ... to carry or convey to heaven without death" (OED). Much like the emphasis on movement in religious translation, *The Martyrology* emphasizes process rather than product. And if translation provides Nichol with a site for foregrounding a subject position in process, it equally offers him a means to negotiate with the mutability of the divine signifier. For Davey, the lines "Lord / the many guises of your signifiers / know you are the signified" in *Book 5* justify God as the "single, permanent, absolute" signified with "multiple and mutable" signifiers. Davey further claims that for Nichol "all language 'games' become significations of the inevitable signified" ("Exegesis" 49). *The Martyrology* certainly grounds itself in the divine, yet its deity is dispersed through language: the more linguistic mutations that the deified "You" undergoes, the "less is known of You" (*Book 5, Chain 3*). When Nichol translates the word "Lord" into the line "l or d" (*Book 4*), he pluralizes the deity and removes it from the status of a substantive object who can be fully present and known. In effect, the contradiction between the meaning of the word "Lord" and its atomized version sets up the deity as the mirror image of the subject in process, marked by pluralities, questions, contradictions.

For Louis Althusser, the traditional Christian deity functions by interpellating subjects "in a double mirror-connexion [sic] such that it *subjects* the subjects to the Subject" (168); because the big S Subject hails individuals into an imaginary relationship with itself and each other, it guarantees the relations of production. However, Nichol's linguistic negations, translations, and dispersals of the deity ensure that readers never see his specular meta-Subject as a stable entity, or the sort of secure point that Althusser posits as a centre for social coherence. While it is true that *The Martyrology* desires a meta-Subject, the insecurity of that Subject in language is reminiscent of the un-representable diety of "negative" theology, where the divine is apprehended through denial rather than through identification.[1] Nichol's translation of a deity into a language which is unable to signify that deity is thus analogous to what Mark C. Taylor has labelled the "de-negation" of negative theology—i.e., "an un-negation that affirms rather than negates negation" ("Non" 2). The theological knowledge constructed by Nichol's text is a non-knowledge, an "agnosis" which supports a divinity who cannot be known or experienced as an objectified presence, but who nevertheless exists as a contradiction.

# U tanikki

carry the poem forward
journal
            the *utanikki*
....
'bp'
'nick the prick'
'pussy'
'nicky'
all of them me
all noted in my *nikki*
adrift between the signifier & the signified
sliding through the years
myself as definition changing (*Book 5, Chain 3*)

The *utanikki* is a Japanese form of personal diary, distinguished by its alternations between poetry and prose, its concern with process and the passage of time, its rejection of the need for daily entries, and its fictionalizing of events. Ann Munton summarizes Earl Miner's "Introduction" to *Japanese Poetic Diaries* (1969), and relates the *utanikki* to Nichol's "tendency to view life in patterns and his exploration of the "processual—time, for instance is not a series of individual events but rather a flow, as the Japanese diarists knew" ("Long" 97). However, McCaffery suggests an alternative reading in his 1988 interview with Nichol:

Juxtapositions, slips, spaces, twists, gaps ... seem the figures of a rhetoric of space which determines *The Martyrology* as a literary object. The work's refusal to assume a panoptic stance and the deliberate eschewal of totality and closure, also suggest its consideration as a major text of space rather than a poetic journal of lived time ("In tens/tion" 87).

Nichol concurs with McCaffery in the same interview: "my applying the term 'utanikki' to my work was a misnaming and, in fact, you were the one who pointed that out to me" (87). True, *The Martyrology* could be considered as a text of space for the reasons enumerated by McCaffery, yet limiting the text to spatial concerns is problematic, because Nichol's blurring of the speech/writing binary occurs precisely because of the temporal, diachronic notation of a chronobiological body, who exists simultaneously in somatic temporality and textual synchrony.[T]

Nichol's "retroactive" discovery of the *utanikki* as a poetic model has received much commentary.[31] However, little critical attention has been given to the relationship between *The Martyrology*'s supposed similarity to the *utanikki* form and its organization of a desiring subject. Perhaps Smaro Kamboureli comes closest to discussing this issue when she writes that *The Martyrology*'s concern with the self is primarily worked out in its various inscriptions of the interrelationships between the singular "i" and the plural "we," and that the lower case "i" "posits a self who is "conscious of its limitations and relative marginality" (99). Her argument could be developed productively in relation to the autobiographical elements of the *utanikki* form by juxtaposing Nichol's self-conscious "i" against Lacan's fading "I." The *utanikki*'s constant formal interruptions destabilize the unicity of conventional autobiography and its construction of the classical subject of knowledge, who can answer with his name or with the word "I" to the question "who is speaking?". In the place of that "I" *The Martyrology* negotiates a self-reflexive subject who exists between personal, autobiographical detail and the socially shared context of language, a self which Nichol represents as being "adrift between the signifier & the signified" (*Book 5, Chain 3*). When Nichol asks "when

---

[31]The most extensive discussions of the *utanikki* form in relation to *The Martyrology* are Munton's "The Long Poem as Poetic Diary" (1985) and "Coming to a Head, 'in a head, ahead' of Us All: Connecting with Book 5" (1988). Irene Niechoda also points out that Nichol's conscious adoption of the *utanikki* occurs in Book 4, although the earlier books were "clearly beginning to take on this kind of rhythm" (169), and Shirley Neuman observes that the "value of the journal for Nichol's undertaking lies in its continuous discontinuities, its circumulativenenss across the 'constant formal interruption' ... that characterizes successive journal entries in general and the *utanikki* model Nichol adopts in particular" (57). Nichol comments on his use of the form: "what you get in the utanikki is a mixture of prose interrupted by poem, interrupted by prose, interrupted by poem, interrupted by prose, and that linkage goes on. Though that is obviously not precisely what happens in *The Martyrology*, what does happen is a constant formal interruption; that is to say, I'm dealing with form this way, then I'm dealing with form that way" ("Syntax" 24).

was it i / quoted myself / into the world" (*Book 6 Books*), the question might be rephrased and answered in Lacanian terms as "I am that which I am not," or in Žižek's reformulation: "I am conscious of myself only insofar as I am out of reach to myself" (*Tarrying* 15). For Lacan, the subject's acquisition of language—quoting itself into the world—enables it to enter the differential fabric of social relations which constitute it as lack. But Nichol foregrounds social relations through the use of proper names, and through the small case "i," in order to offer a "deliberate confrontational device" which will explore the "psychology of the reading experience" (Nichol "In tens/tion" 84). This explorative organization of the desiring subject illustrates how language speaks through a subject whose "I" fades towards the small case "i" as it recognizes its place in a dialectic with the Other. In other words, the implied subject of *The Martyrology* is that which it is not—the "I" is never where it assumes itself to be because it resides simultaneously in the autobiographical details of the *utanikki* form and in the field of the Other.

# Vision: "Hegel's Eyes"

Marjorie Perloff has coined the neologism "poetheory" to describe recent attempts by North American writers to imbricate theoretical and literary texts. Poetheory opposes the desire for "strenuous authenticity, the desire to present a self as natural, as organic, and as unmediated as possible" (*Radical* 20). Unlike "official verse culture" (Bernstein's term for the strenuous authentics), poetheory does not deny historicity, nor does it naturalize and ground itself in transcendent principles.[32] McCaffery's "Hegel's Eyes" (1991) offers a good example of Perloffian poetheory, because it blurs the generic boundaries among prose, poetry, philosophy, and contemporary literary theory. However, the text does not "use" Hegel in the way that a theorist such as Žižek might reconfigure Hegelian ideas in an academic context. Instead, it parodies the language of discursive writing, thereby enacting (as opposed to conveying) a critique of the singular, panoptic viewpoint of a unified self; "Hegel's Eyes" lack of stable representation performatively constructs the subject as text. In the sub-section "Concept Obstinacy in Deep Narrative Structure," for example, McCaffery writes:

If the boat had snapped it was from a dialectical necessity to try. We had been promised taxonomy during the futile dispute over claims, yet the masses to the south had moved a month before our natural causes emerged. I was, however, still in season and according to the ethics of response still guardian of the prior synthesis. So terror touched a new sensation: the plain stupidity of sympathetic contradiction. We had left about noon and as our plan required presented schism

---

[32]More explicitly, Bernstein characterizes the official verse culture of poems and reviews published in mainstream presses such as *The New Yorker* and the *American Poetry Review* as writing which upholds "restricted vocabulary, neutral and univocal tone in the guise of voice or persona, grammar-book syntax, received conceits, static and unitary form. In Williams's terms, writing like this is *used* to convey emotions or ideas rather than allowed to enact them" ("Academy" 245).

as a mock form of the subject. Naming had disappointed, so our resolve was to revise the role of character accumulated in each series (22).

While the passage inscribes character(s) through the pronouns "I," "our," and "we," the narrative refuses to grant stable identity of character through descriptive image or determinate action. Instead, subjectivity is foregrounded as a purely textual sign through indeterminate propositions[o] ("I was, however, still in season"), self-reflexivity ("our resolve was to revise the role of character"), and ungrammatical syntax ("our plan required presented schism"). The "I" is guardian of a "prior synthesis" which is not referred to in the text, unless it is the puzzling *aufhebung* of a boat "snapped" through a "dialectical necessity to try." This series of pictorial and conceptual indeterminacies undercuts rational thought as the support for a unified subject (perhaps the obstinate concept of the sub-title?), while constructing subjectivity as dispersed through language. Foregrounding desire, "Hegel's Eyes" are the eyes of lack; like the Lacanian "scopic drive," they shift continually among signifiers in an unfulfilled attempt to find fully present meaning, and the text thus blinds the classical, transparent subject of knowledge.[33] Instead of constructing an aesthetic based on the assumption of Apollonian lucidity as the ground for unified subjectivity, "Hegel's Eyes" inscribes a non-individuated subject position through Dionysian excess.

In "White Mythology" Derrida demonstrates how metaphor has been the precondition for philosophical truth claims (claims which paradoxi-

---

[33]In *Three Essays on Sexuality* (1905), Freud discusses "*scopophilia*", i.e., the association of looking and being looked at with pleasure. Freud's narrative follows a typical pattern: scopophilia begins in the pre-oedipal phase, when the child blurs the important distinction between the *active* pleasure of looking (voyeurism) and the *passive* pleasure of being looked at (exhibitionism). The child at this stage looks at its own body as if it were an object. However, Freud claims that the active and passive types of scopophilia gradually become distinct, and are codified as masculine and feminine at the Oedipal phase. Following the Oedipal correlation of activity with masculinity and the phallic, and passivity with femininity and castration, voyeurism becomes associated with masculinity, and exhibitionism with femininity (Wright 448). For Lacan, however, the scopic drive is the subject's visual search for an *objet a*, symbol of the lack of the phallus "in so far as it is lacking" (*Four* 103). Like all Lacanian drives, the scopic drive is opposed to the absolute pressure of biological need; Lacan claims that the constancy of the drive's thrust "forbids any assimilation of the drive to a biological function, which always has a rhythm" (*Four* 165).

cally attempt to downgrade metaphor, but which also provide a site for metaphor's theorization). "Hegel's Eyes" similarly foregrounds the centrality of poetic language within discursive prose. This approach becomes evident when we consider the text's tendency to shift between theoretical language and pictorial image, as in the following sentences: "Proper in the tautological sense of proper plus the sky is not grey" (11); "Content slides, detected as enlarged, then disenclosed in a further sheath device" (15); "The plausibility of psychoanalytic modification hints a proximal place among ruins" (42). The fragmented surfaces of these sentences deconstruct the opposition between theoretical discourse and the sensuous material of pictorial imagery. Because of its predominant concentration on the sensuousness of the signifier at the expense of content, the text is an Idea-free zone. However, the predominance of its various theoretical traces suggest that it is more concerned with content than with form—albeit a highly indeterminate content. The text does not resolve these differences as a classical balance between form and content, but maintains them as incommensurable contradictions. The text thus follows McCaffery's Bataillian claim that general economy regards the barrier between antitheses as an "actual target for dissolution, whose removal then allows the abolition of both terms as separate identities" (*North* 213). For McCaffery the *aufhebung* is a restrictive operation to the extent that it preserves antithetical elements through synthesis; like restricted economy, the dialectic ensures that "nothing is wasted and profit is squeezed out of every negative labour" (*North* 212). McCaffery regards general economy as a means to oppose the metaphysics of the *aufhebung*, because general economy attacks the bar between antithetical terms by operating "towards break-down and discharge rather than accumulation and integration" (213). As a writing through the expenditures of general economy, "Hegel's Eyes" spills the sensible into the intelligible—and vice versa—thereby ensuring that the text has value only as writing, and not as a representation of transcendent principles.

# Writing with Xerox

you take a text and duplicate it, then duplicate the duplication, then duplicate the duplication of the duplication systematically with exact 'duplication' never occurring. there's always visual change, textual shift—an insistence on the piece's emergent self and through the agency of the mechanical means of composition an insistence on the piece's *uniqueness at every stage* (*Rational* 142; emphasis added).

McCaffery claims that Walter Benjamin's "The Work of Art in the Age of Mechanical Reproduction" (1935) was the "theoretical inspiration" behind his work with photo copiers, which he labels as "xeroxography" ("Annotated" 86). For Benjamin, the mechanical reproduction of aesthetic texts eliminates the "aura" of that text—i.e., that supposedly authentic "essence of all that is transmissible from its beginning" (223). Because the technique of reproduction substitutes a potentially infinite number of copies for a unique existence, it causes the aura of the original text to "wither" (223). Benjamin suggests that the desire of contemporary masses to overcome "the uniqueness of every reality by accepting its reproduction" (225) leads art away from its traditional ritualistic function (including the "cult of beauty"), thereby transforming art into a potential site for class emancipation. However, the TRG's version of xeroxography constructs the reproduced text as an object that is unique at every stage. Their insistence works against Benjamin's argument by conceiving of every version of the reproduced object as an original; in effect, the TRG returns the aura to the reproduction. Mechanical reproduction is not for the TRG a means to create similarities, but a means to generate differences, and by considering writing through xerox in terms of its capacity to duplicate a duplication of a duplication, the TRG construct all duplications as authentically unique. Moreover, the second panel of McCaffery's *Carnival*—a text that employs a number of forms, including "xeroxography within xeroxography (i.e. metaxeroxography and disintegrative seriality)"—further emphasizes a desire for authenticity that seems counter-productive to Benjamin's project:

The roots of *Carnival* go beyond concretism (specifically that particular branch of concrete poetry termed the 'typestract' or abstract typewriter art) to labyrinth and mandala, and all related archetypal forms the emphasize the use of the visual qualities in language to defend a sacred centre (n.p.).

McCaffery here reinforces the type of ritualistic function[G] for art that Benjamin considers to be oppositional to the emancipated character of mechanical reproduction. For Benjamin, the disappearance of the auratic remnants of ritual allows aesthetic texts to be interpreted and evaluated according to socio-political relations. Although McCaffery claimed a decade after the TRG report that his early xerox compositions were inspired by Benjamin's stress on the political aspects of reproduction—the "modes of production in a mass market economy" ("Annotated" 86)—both his own early theory of "metaxeroxography" as a "means to defend a sacred centre" and the TRG's collaborative analysis of xeroxo-graphy unconsciously de-politicize mechanical reproduction by returning the aesthetic object to the tradition of authenticity.

Given the Benjaminian foundations of the TRG's writing on xerox composition, their use of the phrase "uniqueness at every stage" illustrates a gap between on the one hand xeroxography as political challenge to the decontextualized aesthetic object (à la Benjamin), and on the other hand, a quasi-theological desire for the One of complete and authentic presence. Perhaps this gap unconsciously sets up McCaffery's 1986 comment that xeroxography was relevant to his interest in general economy:

There was something of a festive expenditure and a sacrificial logic at work in these process pieces. The mechanical reproduction of a loss; the transformation of sign into noise; the cavalier discard of information and the movement away from an order of symbolization to a gestural, material level of pre-linguistic substance ("Annotated" 87).

Although McCaffery directly refers to the loss that occurs through xeroxographic process, the indeterminate no-man's land formed between the One and the many in the Group's earlier discussion is unconsciously consistent with the contradictory, double disposition that is central to McCaffery's later reading of Bataille.

McCaffery ties his interest in xeroxography to the "problematics of repetition" ("Annotated" 86). Much like his work on translation, he does not conceive of writing with xerox as a movement of modified informa-tion from a source text to a target text, but as a means to generate a series of entirely new texts. Benjamin and Lacan both offer a critique of origins, albeit from radically different directions. But unlike Benjamin's thesis that reproduction offers a revolutionary challenge to the art work as original aura, Lacan constructs repetition as arising from the subject's failed desire to return to origins. For Lacan, the unconscious *is* repetition: "you repeat because you have not fulfilled your aim" (Miller "Context" 13). McCaffery's xerox compositions unconsciously model this Lacanian economy, because their endless duplication of duplications, without reference to an initial text, illustrates the impossibility of returning to an origin by a subjectivity that is entirely constituted through deferral.

# Yin-Yang

In *Seminar XI* Lacan claims Chinese science inscribes the "reality of the heavens ... in nothing more than a vast constellation of signifiers" that are based on oppositions such as "Yin and Yang, water and fire, hot and cold" (*Four* 151). These oppositions are "motivated by the sexual divisions of society"; for Lacan, the signifier "came into the world" through the binary structure of "sexual reality" (*Four* 151). Like Lacan, Nichol does not hesitate to use concepts drawn from Chinese culture as metaphors for his theory of language. In a TRG note labelled "Interstate 75—120 miles from Tampa, October 2/74," he writes: "the fluid nature of the relationship between signifier & signified—what Lacan meant about the one sliding beneath the other—this ties in to the yin-yang balance—any signifier is always relative to what it signifies" (*Rational* 195). Nichol's construction of a link between Taoist philosophy and Lacanian theory begs meditation, because unlike Lacan's writings on language which typically centre on absence, lack and desire, Nichol's imbrication of Lacan with Taoist yin-yang suggests a far more holistic conception of language. Nichol re-orients Lacan by sublating linguistic opposition under the sign of balance, thereby returning antithetical terms to a single point of definition. Remember that Taoism represents the antagonism between yin and yang in the emblem of a circle divided into equal fields of black and white, with a small dot of one colour embedded in its opposite field. As an illustration of balanced wholeness, this sign constructs the interaction of opposing forces within the closed constraints of a circular field; paradoxically, the circularity of Taoist philosophy subsumes difference into singularity, and exclusion into an objectified and inclusive whole. In "The *Tao* and the *Logos*: Notes on Derrida's Critique of Logocentrism" (1985), Zhang Longxi points out that the language of Taoism is logocentric to the extent that it emphasizes "the inadequacy and even futility of writing" (392). Wei Yuan, a 19th century commentator on Taoism, explains that the "*tao* cannot be manifested through language" (qtd. in Longxi 392). Although the counter-culture "cosmic" connotations of

Nichol's use of Taoist discourse emerge more explicitly in his earlier writing,[34] the tao as a site of logocentrism is still present as a trace structure within the fragment quoted above. By aligning Lacan's theory of language with a sublation of antithetical terms through the concept of yin-yang balance, Nichol constructs a misprision of Lacan, for his creative misreading uncritically misrecognizes the tao as an attainable object of desire.

Kristeva briefly cites the "Yin-Yang 'dialogue'" as an example of a philosophy which goes beyond the monologic limitations of singularity (*Desire* 69), and suggests that the dialogic ambivalence of poetic language is shared by the tao. Of course, to read the tao as a dialogue is to undo my earlier argument, which conceives of yin-yang balance as a sublation of opposing terms into a singular object of desire. Re-contextualizing Hegel's definition of the *aufhebung*, we could say that the tao is "the same word for two opposite meanings" (*Science* 107), because the yin-yang economy is not a stable entity, but an instance of unfinalizable dialogue. The multivalency of the term thus destabilizes the unity of definition that Kristeva associates with logic and scientific abstraction. She argues that all logical systems based on a "zero-one sequence (true false, nothingness-notation)" are unable to "account for the operation of poetic language" (*Desire* 70). While Nichol may not have been aware of what his note's short connection between Lacan and *Taoism* might potentially offer its readers, the doubleness that ensues between lack (existing as a trace in the theory and name of Lacan) and yin-yang balance (connoting wholeness in balance) provides us with a typical example of his poetics, which frequently focuses on doubleness rather than on the logic of either/or. Nichol's misprision of Lacan is not so much a misrecognition of presence

---

[34]Irene Niechoda glosses the lines: "for friendship's sake my house is set / the blue dragon on my right / the white tiger on my left" in *Book 2* of *The Martyrology* in regard to John Mitchell's *The New View Over Atlantis* (1969), a text which Nichol read while writing the second book. Mitchell claims that magnetic force was known in ancient China as the "dragon current," and that it consisted of "yin and yang, negative and positive, represented by the white tiger and the blue dragon.... The most favourable position is where the two streams meet" (qtd. in Niechoda 145-6). Mitchell's text is concerned with several discourses that were enjoyed by the flower-children, including the myth of Atlantis, the mythologization of Asia, the desire to return to a pre-modern circuit of balanced nature, the pseudo-science of geomancy, and *Taoist* philosophy.

that is fully complicit with the desires of the Other (i.e. the desire to be desired), but a carnivalesque challenge to the structural logic of the subject-Other dialectic, based as that dialectic is on a zero-one sequence of lack and desire. The text's contradiction of terms transgresses logocentrism, thereby contaminating symbolic law with semiotic ambivalence.

# Zarathrustran 'Pataphysics

As the last letter, should Z reiterate the alphabet? Should it complete the letters by synthesizing meaning, answering possible questions and objections, and setting up goals for future research? Nichol writes, "the trouble with conclusions is that they conclude" ("Things" 148); to conclude is to construct a final determination, to arrive at a judgement by reasoning, to close the question: "the conclusyoun is a clarkeley gatherynge of the matter spoken before." But instead of constructing a decisive summary, why not put together a concluding un-scientific postscript? A 'pataphysical description of a conclusion, based on the TRG's own inscriptions of 'pataphysics and "pataphysics?

Building on Alfred Jarry's definition of 'pataphysics as: "the science of imaginary solutions" (193), the Group define Canadian "Pataphysics as "the literature of all imaginary sciences" (*Rational* 302). In Jarry's orthography of the word, 'pataphysics

should be preceded by an apostrophe so as to avoid a simple pun [*patte à physique* is the French word for the child's game 'patty-cake'] . . . ['pataphysics] is "the science of that which is superinduced upon metaphysics, whether within or beyond the latter's limitations, extending as far beyond metaphysics as the latter extends beyond physics (192).

The TRG's introduction to the *Canadian "Pataphysics* issue of *Open Letter* (1979) extends Jarry's definition by arguing that a specifically Canadian "pataphysics is not a

'pataphysics at all, but rather a superinducement on the superinducement. Nothing less than a Canadian "Pataphysics. Not 'Pata-physics but rather "Pata-physics... The distinction is subtle: from elision (') to quotation (") through a superinducement on elision ('+' = ") (*Rational* 301).

By shifting from the elision of the apostrophe to the superinducement of a double apostrophe that is indicated as a quotation mark, the TRG institute "a science of the perpetually open citing," in order to question the "given that we do not understand but with emendations that serve to constitute our explanation" (301-2). As a science which self-reflexively constructs its own explanations and observations as fictions, Canadian "Pataphysics parodies expository discourse.

Linda Hutcheon reminds us that parody is "repetition with critical distance" ("Theory" 6). Nichol's various "Probable Systems," published in *Zygal: A Book of Mysteries and Translations* (1980) and *art facts: a book of contexts* (1990), provide a good example of "Pataphysics. In "Probable System 19" (1973-74, 1988) for instance, Nichol constructs a "formula for determining a reader's ability to gain access to the book/machine" (*art* 64). He designates P as the "degree of adherence to, or antipathy towards, traditional book/machine values on the part of the reader," C as the degree to which the "book/machine is utilized tradition-ally or in a non-traditional way by the writer," and A as the "reader's ability to gain access to the book/machine" (64). P and C are also rated on a scale of 1 to 10; for P, 1 represents complete antipathy and 10 complete acceptance of traditional book machine values, while for C, 1 represents traditional utilization and 10 a radical departure from the book/machine. To someone who is easily confused by numbers (such as myself), the system is bewildering, although it still verges on logic. The formula for determining the reader's ability to gain access to the book-machine is "$100 (10/P(C)) = A$," and Nichol provides a model of this formula in operation:

Fred (a traditionalist rated 10 on the P scale) reads the latest Arthur Hailey novel (rating of 1 on the C scale).
*computation*
$$100 (10/P(C)) = A$$
$$100 (10/10(1)) = 100 (10/10) = 100 (1/1)$$
$$= 100$$
A = 100% access for Fred to Arthur Hailey's novel (65).

These computations parody the rigour of a science by repeating the scientific form and language of an equation. "Probable Systems 19" parallels Jarry's 'pataphysical investigation of scientific imagination by presenting an absurd and seemingly arbitrary mathematical formula, thereby parodically challenging the scientific construction of truth.

McCaffery's 1997 essay "Zarathrustran 'Pataphysics" is similarly an imaginary science, although instead of repeating mathematical science with a critical distance it parodies the "science" of literary criticism. The text begins in a relatively lucid manner: "Let us initially envision (before discarding it) a Lucianic dialogue (of sorts) conducted entirely in Jarry's terms..." (11), but then becomes increasingly opaque due to orthographical errors, citing such texts as the *"Potable Netzsche"* (14) and "Max Olow's isympetries fron *Stanzas for Irid Lexak"* (18),[35] until it reaches its concluding sentence:

A more Neezstchan ingageamen must forgrunod the texts' soveriegn enternaxity and insiss upon an effactive reading, bt wat of Zatarushton 'Pataphyusixs, demsnding synboloc afgirmation of the wroding's nihilitdic impligatiuns, espellciary tho inputei loas of boat radear ans wrirer befoer the paralogycs of the machome within sygn effevct that refute to ve consyned, comprhendd, or dimsmiszed (22).

"Zarathrustran 'Pataphysics" borrows and modifies sections from McCaffery's critical work on American poet Jackson Mac Low,[36] as well as from writings by Nietzsche, Deleuze and Guattari, Derrida, Kristeva, and others. The paragrammatic word "thrust" embedded in "Zarathrustra" is no accident; recall the TRG's claim that the "referential thrust" of content connect "a highly complex inter-textual network" (*Rational* 134).[1] Yet McCaffery performatively de-stabilizes these recognizable intertexts by drawing our attention to the material surface of the signifier. Because the essay's referential qualities engage with its non-referential features, it parallels Kristeva's writings on the subject existing as a split between mutually interactive symbolic and semiotic categories. As we have seen, this interaction is central to McCaffery's writing. And as a general economy, the text foregrounds the loss of meaning over the transmission of a recognizable message from literary critic to reader. Much like the "pataphysical dimension of Nichol's "Probable Systems," as well as the playful approach to research suggested by the TRG reports,[JM] "Zarathrustran 'Pataphysics" occupies a place in the literature of imaginary science.

If the imaginary science of "pataphysics as practised by the TRG is a general economy, it contests commodity culture's stress on productive use value. As Lyotard writes,

The relationship of the suppliers and users of knowledge to the knowledge they supply and use is now tending, and will increasingly tend, to assume the form already taken by the relationship of commodity producers and consumers to the

---

[35]*The Portable Nietzsche* and Jackson Mac Low's *Asymmetries* from *Stanzas for Iris Lezak.*

[36]"Jackson Mac Low:   Samsara in Lagado" (1987) and "Mac Low's *Asymmetries"* (1986).

commodities they produce—that is, the form of use value. Knowledge is and will be produced in order to be sold, it is and will be consumed in order to be valorized in a new production: in both cases the goal is exchange (*Postmodern* 4).

Unlike the use-oriented goals attributed by Lyotard to commodified knowledge, the TRG construct a useless "pataphysics that expends knowledge. By parodying specific forms of knowledge, the Group seem to provide a counter-discourse to the power/knowledge complex. Or do they? Jameson's claim that the production of aesthetic form is "an ideological act in its own right, with the function of inventing imaginary or formal 'solutions' to unresolvable social contradictions" (*Political* 79) calls into question the politics of the Group's legitimation of a "science of imaginary solutions" and a "literature of all imaginary sciences." If the purely formal act of constructing an imaginary resolution occurs as a misrecognition of the unresolvable conditions of social existence, "pataphysics would seem to be one of the least politically challenging of the TRG's endeavors. However, the Group's tendency to optimistically construct theory and formally innovative literature as sites for free-play ruptures established forms of inquiry. Even though their "pataphyscial musings may be a misrecognition, they provide a serious intervention into the history of research in the Canadian literary context.

And if this "pataphysical conclusion to *ABC of Reading TRG* is similarly a literature of the imaginary solution, what does it imagine? McCaffery's and Nichol's heterogeneous approaches to writing—both as collaborators and alone—make their texts exceptional sites for dialogue, for intertextual misprision, and for reflecting on questions rather than for producing answers. The dialogic quality of the Group's work provides an active site for a critical sub-culture to organize its own enjoyment, in relation to the cultural practices of formal innovation. These specific forms of enjoyment materialize not only through the TRG's interrogation of the politics of reference and reading, but also through their spanning of conversational and theoretical poles of discourse, their humour and earnestness, and their "pataphysical imagination.

# Works Cited

Ahearn, Barry. *Zukofsky's "A": An Introduction*. Berkeley: U of California P, 1983.

Althusser, Louis. "Ideology and the Ideological State Apparatuses." 1970. *Lenin and Philosophy*. Trans. Ben Brewster. New York: Monthly Review P, 1971. 123-173.

Andrews, Bruce, Charles Bernstein, Ray Di Palma, Steve McCaffery, Ron Silliman. *LEGEND*. New York: L=A=N=G=U=A=G=E/Segue, 1980.

Bakhtin, M.M. *The Dialogic Imagination*. Trans. Michael Holquist. Austin: U of Texas P, 1981.

Banting, Pamela. "The Body as Pictogram: Rethinking Hélène Cixous's Ecriture Féminine." *Textual Practice* 6.1 (1992): 225-246.

Barbour, Douglas. "bpNichol" *Canadian Writers and Their Works*. Ed. Robert Lecker, Jack David, and Ellen Quigley. Vol. 8. Poetry series. Toronto: ECW P, 1992. 263-357.

Barreto-Rivera, Rafael. "Dr. Sadhu's Semi-Opticks, or How to Write a Virtual-Novel by the Book: Steve McCaffery's *Panopticon*." *Open Letter* 6.9 (1987): 39-47.

Barthes, Roland. "The Death of the Author." 1968. Trans. Stephen Heath. *Image - Music - Text*. New York: Hill and Wang, 1977. 142-164.

_____. *S/Z*. 1970. Trans. Richard Miller. New York: Hill and Wang, 1974.

_____. *The Pleasure of the Text*. 1973. Trans. Richard Miller. New York: Hill and Wang, 1975.

Bataille, Georges. *Literature and Evil*. 1957. Trans. Alastair Hamilton. London: Calder and Boyars, 1973.

_____. *Visions of Excess: Selected Writings, 1927-1939*. Ed. and Trans. Allan Stoekl. Minneapolis: U of Minnesota P, 1985.

Baudrillard, Jean. *Simulations*. Trans. Paul Foss, Paul Patton, and Philip Beitchman. New York: Semiotext(e), 1983

Bayard, Caroline. "Deux pièces difficiles pour une même main." *ellipse* 23-24 (1979): 156-173.

_____. *The New Poetics in Canada and Quebec: From Concretism to Post-Modernism*. Toronto: U of Toronto P, 1989.

Benjamin, Walter. "The Work of Art in the Age of Mechanical Reproduction." 1935. Trans. Harry Zohn. *Illuminations*. New York: Schocken Books, 1969. 217-251.

Bentley, D.M.R. "Introduction." *Abram's Plains: A Poem*. London: Canadian Poetry P, 1986. xi-xlviii.

Benveniste, Emile. *Problems in General Linguistics*. 1966. Trans. Mary Elizabeth Meek. Coral Gables: U of Miami P, 1971.

Bernstein, Charles. "The Academy in Peril: William Carlos Williams meets the MLA." 1983. *Content's Dream: Essays 1975-1984*. Los Angeles: Sun and Moon P, 1986. 244-251.

____. "An Autobiographical Interview with Charles Bernstein." With Loss Pequeño Glazier. *Boundary 2* 23.3 (1996): 21-43.

____. *A Poetics*. London: Harvard UP, 1992.

Blodgett, E.D. "Foreword." *Prefaces and Literary Manifestos / Préfaces et manifestes littéraires*. Ed. E.D. Blodgett and A.G. Purdy. HOLIC * HILAC Research Institute for Comparative Literature: U of Alberta, 1990. ix-xv.

Bloom, Harold. *Kabbalah and Criticism*. New York: Seabury P, 1975.

Bök, Christian. "Nor the Fun Tension: Steve McCaffery and his critical 'Paradoxy'." *Open Letter* 8.3 (1992): 90-103.

Bök, Christian, and Darren Wershler-Henry. "*Carnival*, a Bipartite Mural and Concrete Poem by Steve McCaffery." Eye Rhymes: A Multidisciplinary, International Conference on Visual Poetry. Edmonton, Alberta. June 13, 1997.

Bowering, George, ed. *The Contemporary Canadian Poem Anthology*. Toronto: Coach House P, 1983.

Brant, Beth. "Whose Voice is it Anyway?: A Symposium on Who Should be Speaking for Whom." *Books in Canada* 20.1 (1991): 12.

Burnham, Clint. "Re Reading: A Commentary on Book 5, Chain 7." *Tracing the Paths*. Ed. Roy Miki. Vancouver: Talonbooks, 1988. 204-212.

Butling, Pauline. "bpNichol's Gestures in *Book 6 Books*." *Tracing the Paths*. Ed. Roy Miki. Vancouver: Talonbooks, 1988. 237-259.

Cary, Thomas. *Abram's Plains: A Poem*. 1789. London: Canadian Poetry P, 1986.

Clark, David L. "Monstrous Reading: *The Martyrology* After De Man." *Studies in Canadian Literature*. 15.2 (1990): 1-32.

Coffey, Michael. "Grammatology & Economy." *Open Letter* 6.9 (1987): 27-38.

Davey, Frank. *Canadian Literary Power*. Edmonton: NeWest P, 1994.

____. "Exegesis / Eggs à Jesus; *The Martyrology* as a Text in Crisis." *Tracing the Paths*. Ed. Roy Miki. Vancouver: Talonbooks, 1988. 38-51.

____. "Rime, A Scholarly Piece." 1965. *The Making of Modern Poetry in Canada*. Ed. Louis Dudek and Michael Gnarowsky. Toronto: Ryerson P, 1967. 295-300.

David, Jack and Robert Lecker, eds. *Canadian Poetry*. Vol. 2. New Press Canadian Classics. Toronto: Stoddart, 1994.

Deleuze, Gilles, and Felix Guattari. *Anti-Oedipus: Capitalism and Schizophrenia*. 1977. Trans. Robert Hurley, Mark Seem, Helen R. Lane. New York: Viking, 1983.

____. "Introduction: Rhizome." *A Thousand Plateaus: Capitalism and Schizophrenia*. 1980. Trans. Brian Massumi. Minneapolis: Minnesota UP, 1987. 3-27.

De Man, Paul. "Hypogram and Inscription." 1981. *The Resistance to Theory*. Theory and History of Literature, Vol. 33. Minneapolis: U of Minnesota P, 1986. 27-53.

____. "Intentional Structure of the Romantic Image." *The Rhetoric of Romanticism*. New York: Columbia UP, 1984. 1-17.

Derksen, Jeff. "Mapping Mind, Mapping Frames: *The Martyrology* and its Social Text." *Beyond the Orchard: Essays on The Martyrology*. Ed. Roy Miki and Fred Wah. Vancouver: West Coast Line, 1997.

Derrida, Jacques. *Writing and Difference*. 1967. Trans. Alan Bass. Chicago: U of Chicago P, 1978.

____. *Of Grammatology*. 1967. Trans. Gayatri Chakravorty Spivak. Baltimore: Johns Hopkins UP, 1976.

____. "White Mythology: Metaphor in the Text of Philosophy." 1971. *Margins of Philosophy*. Trans. Alan Bass. Chicago: U of Chicago P, 1982.

Dutton, Paul and Steven Smith, ed. *Read the Way he Writes: A Festschrift for bpNichol*. *Open Letter* 6.5-6 (1986).

____. "The Sonic Graffitist: Steve McCaffery as Improviser." *Open Letter* 6.9 (1987): 17-25.

Eagleton, Terry. *Literary Theory: An Introduction*. Minneapolis: U of Minnesota p, 1983.

Edelstein, Marilyn. "Toward a Feminist Postmodern Poléthique: Kristeva on Ethics and Politics." *Ethics, Politics, and Difference in Julia Kristeva's Writing*. Ed. Kelly Oliver. New York: Routledge, 1993.

196-214.

Felman, Shoshana. *Jacques Lacan and the Adventure of Insight: Psycho-analysis in Contemporary Culture.* Cambridge: Harvard UP, 1987.

Finlay, Ian Hamilton. "Letter to Pierre Garnier." 1963. *Concrete Poetry: A World View.* Ed. Mary Ellen Solt. Bloomington: Indiana UP, 1968. 84.

Foucault, Michel. "Nietzsche, Genealogy, History." 1971. *language, counter-memory, practice.* Ed. Donald F. Bouchard. Ithaca, Cornell UP, 1977. 139-164.

____. *The Order of Things.* 1966. New York: Vintage, 1970.

Four Horsemen. *CaNADAda.* Toronto: Griffin House, 1972.

Freud, Sigmund. "A Note Upon the 'Mystic Writing Pad'." 1921. *The Standard Edition of the Complete Psychological Works.* Vol 19. Trans James Strachey. London: Hogarth P, 1953. 227-232.

____. *Three Essays on the Theory of Sexuality.* 1905. *The Standard Edition of the Complete Psychological Works.* Vol. 7. Trans. James Strachey. London: Hogarth Press, 1953. 125-245.

Gallop, Jane. *Reading Lacan.* Ithaca: Cornell UP, 1985.

Geddes, Gary, ed. *20th Century Poetry and Poetics.* 2nd ed. Toronto: Oxford UP, 1973.

Gomringer, Eugen. "silencio." 1953. *Concrete Poetry: A World View.* Ed. Mary Ellen Solt. Bloomington: Indiana UP, 1968. 91.

Grant, Iain Hamilton. "Glossary." *Libidinal Economy.* 1974. Trans. Iain Hamilton Grant. Bloomington: Indiana UP, 1993. x-xvi.

Hart, Kevin. *The Trespass of the Sign: Deconstruction, Theology and Philosophy.* Cambridge: Cambridge UP, 1989.

Hartley, George. *Textual Politics and the Language Poets.* Bloomington: Indiana UP, 1989.

Hegel, G. W.F. *Science of Logic.* Trans. A.V. Miller. London: Allen and Unwin, 1969.

Henderson, Brian. "New Syntaxes in McCaffery and Nichol: Emptiness, Transformation, Serenity." *Essays on Canadian Writing* 37 (1989): 1-29.

____. "Radical Poetics: Dada, bpNichol, and the Horsemen." Diss. York U, 1982.

Hindley-Smith, Lee, Stan Kutz, Philip McKenna and bpNichol. "Thera-fields." *Canadian Forum* (Jan. 1973): 12-17.

Holquist, Michael. "Bakhtin and the Body." *Critical Studies* 1.2 (1989): 19-42.

Hutcheon, Linda. *The Canadian Postmodern*. Toronto: Oxford UP, 1988.
_____. *A Theory of Parody*. New York: Methuen, 1985.
Jabés, Edmond. *The Book of Questions*. 1963. Trans. Rosmarie Waldrop. Middletown: Wesleyan UP, 1976.
Jacobus, Mary. "Anna (Wh)O.'s *Absences*: Readings in Hysteria." *Reading Woman: Essays in Feminist Criticism*. New York: Columbia UP, 1986. 195-274.
Jakobson, Roman. "On Linguistic Aspects of Translation." *On Translation*. Ed. R.A. Brower. Cambridge: Harvard UP, 1959. 232-239.
Jameson, Fredric. *Marxism and Form*. Princeton: Princeton UP, 1971.
_____. *The Political Unconscious*. Ithaca: Cornell UP, 1981.
_____. "Postmodernism and Consumer Society." *The Anti-Aesthetic*. Ed. Hal Foster. Port Townsend: Bay P, 1983. 111-125.
Janov, Arthur. "The Levels of Consciousness." *Primal Man: The New Consciousness*. Arthur Janov and E. Michael Holden. New York: Thomas Y. Crowell, 1975. 79-111.
Jarry, Alfred. *Selected Works of Alfred Jarry*. Ed. Roger Shattuck and Simon Watson Taylor. London: Methuen, 1965.
Jay, Martin. *Downcast Eyes: The Denigration of Vision in Twentieth-Century French Thought*. Berkeley: U of California P, 1994.
Joy, Morny. "Conclusion: Divine Reservations." *Derrida and Negative Theology*. Ed. Harold Coward and Toby Foshay. Albany: SUNY P, 1992. 255-282.
Kamboureli, Smaro. "'there's so much i': Self and Genre in *The Martyrology*. *Tracing the Paths*. Ed. Roy Miki. Vancouver: Talonbooks, 1988. 95-117.
Kempton, Karl. Untitled. 1992. *CORE: A Symposium on Contemporary Visual Poetry*. Ed. John Byrum and Crag Hill. Mentor / Mill Valley: Generatorscore P, 1993.
Knabb, Ken., ed. and trans. *Situationist International Anthology*. Berkeley: Bureau of Public Secrets, 1981.
Knight, Alan R. "Growing Hegemonies: Preparing the Ground for Official Anthologies of Canadian Poetry." *Prefaces and Literary Manifestos / Préfaces et manifestes littéraires*. Ed. E.D. Blodgett and A.G. Purdy. HOLIC * HILAC Research Institute for Comparative Literature: U of Alberta, 1990. 146-157.
_____. "The Toronto Research Group Reports: A Myth of Textuality." *Line* 5 (1985): 90-103.
Kristeva, Julia. *Desire in Language*. 1977. Ed. Leon S. Roudiez. Trans.

Thomas Gora, Alice Jardine, and Leon S. Roudiez. New York: Columbia UP, 1980.

____. *Powers of Horror*. 1980. Trans. Leon S. Roudiez. New York: Columbia UP, 1982.

____. *Revolution in Poetic Language*. 1974. Trans. Margaret Waller. New York: Columbia UP, 1984.

____. *Tales of Love*. 1983. Trans. Leon S. Roudiez. New York: Columbia UP, 1987.

____. "Within the Microcosm of 'The Talking Cure'." 1981. *Interpreting Lacan*. Ed. Joseph Smith and William Kerrigan. New Haven: Yale UP, 1983. 33-48.

Lacan, Jacques. *Ecrits: A Selection*. Trans. Alan Sheridan. New York: W.W. Norton & Co, 1977.

____. *Feminine Sexuality*. Ed. Juliet Mitchell and Jacqueline Rose. Trans. Jacqueline Rose. New York: W.W. Norton & Co, 1982.

____. *The Four Fundamental Concepts of Psycho-Analysis*. Trans. Alan Sheridan. New York: W.W. Norton & Co, 1977.

____. "Seminar on 'The Purloined Letter'." 1956. Trans. Jeffrey Mehlman. *Yale French Studies* 48 (1972): 38-72.

Longxi, Zhang. "The *Tao* and the *Logos*: Notes on Derrida's Critique of Logocentrism." *Critical Inquiry* 11 (1985): 385-397.

Lyotard, Jean-François. *Libidinal Economy*. 1974. Trans. Iain Hamilton Grant. Bloomington: Indiana UP, 1993.

____. *The Postmodern Condition: A Report on Knowledge*. 1979. Trans. Geoff Bennington and Brian Massumi. Minneapolis: Minnesota UP, 1984.

Marcus, Greil. *Lipstick Traces: A Secret History of the Twentieth Century*. Cambridge: Harvard UP, 1989.

Marx, Karl. "The Fetishism of Commodities and the Secret Thereof." 1867. *The Marx-Engels Reader*. Ed. Robert C. Tucker. Trans. Samuel Moore and Edward Aveling. New York: W.W. Norton & Co, 1972. 215-225.

McCaffery, Steve. "The Annotated, Anecdoted, Beginnings of a Critical Checklist of the Published Works of Steve McCaffery." Interview with bpNichol. *Open Letter* 6.9 (1987): 67-92.

____. "Anti-Phonies." Rev. of Fred Wah's *Pictograms from the Interior of B.C. Open Letter* 3.5 (1976): 87-92.

____. *The Black Debt*. London: Nightwood Editions, 1989.

____. *Carnival: The First Panel 1967-70*. Toronto: Coach House P, 1973.

____. *Carnival: The Second Panel 1971-75*. Toronto: Coach House P, 1977.

____. "Critical Responsibilities." *Books in Canada* 19.9 (1990): 24-25.

____. "The Death of the Subject: The Implications of Counter-Communication in Recent Language-Centred Writing." *Open Letter* 3.7 (1977): 61-77.

____. *Dr. Sadhu's Muffins*. Erin: Press Porcepic, 1974.

____. *Evoba: The Investigations Meditations 1976-78*. Toronto: Coach House P, 1987.

____. "An Interview with Steve McCaffery on the TRG." With Peter Jaeger. *Open Letter. bpNichol + 10* 10.4 (1998): 77-96.

____. "Intraview." 1978. *The L=A=N=G=U=A=G=E Book*. Ed. Bruce Andrews and Charles Bernstein. Carbondale: Southern Illinois UP, 1984. 189.

____. "Jackson Mac Low: Samsara in Lagado." *North Dakota* Quarterly 55.4 (1987): 185-201.

____. *North Of Intention*. Toronto: Nightwood Editions, 1986.

____. *'Ow's "waif": and other poems*. Toronto: Coach House P, 1975.

____. *Panopticon*. Toronto: blewointment P, 1984.

____. *The Scenarios*. Toronto: League of Canadian Poets, 1980.

____. *Theory of Sediment*. Vancouver: Talonbooks, 1991.

____. "The Unreadable Text." 1983. *Code of Signals: Recent Writings in Poetics*. Ed. Michael Palmer. Berkeley: North Atlantic Books, 1983. 219-223.

____. "Voice in Extremis." *Close Listening: Poetry and the Performed Word*. Ed. Charles Bernstein. Oxford: Oxford UP, 1998. 162-177.

____. "Zarathrustran 'Pataphysics." *Open Letter* 9.7 (1997): 11-22.

McCaffery, Steve, and bpNichol. *In England Now That Spring*. Toronto: Aya P, 1979.

____. *Rational Geomancy: The Kids of the Book-Machine*. Vancouver: Talonbooks, 1992.

____, eds. *Sound Poetry: A Catalogue for the Eleventh International Sound Poetry Festival, Toronto, Canada, October 14-21, 1978*. Toronto: Underwhich Editions, 1979.

Messerli, Douglas. "Introduction." *"Language" Poetries: An Anthology*. Ed. Douglas Messerli. New York: New Directions, 1987. 1-11.

Miki, Roy, ed. *Tracing the Paths*. Vancouver: Talonbooks, 1988.

Miller, Jacques Alain. "Context and Concepts." *Reading Seminar XI: Lacan's Four Fundamental Concepts of Psychoanalysis*. Ed. Richard

Feldstein, Bruce Fink, Marie Janus. Albany: SUNY P, 1995. 3-15.

Miller, J. Hillis. *The Ethics of Reading: Kant, de Man, Eliot, Trollope, James, and Benjamin*. The Wellek Library Lectures at the University of California, Irvine. New York: Columbia UP, 1987.

Miner, Earl. "Introduction." *Japanese Poetic Diaries*. Berkeley and Los Angeles: U of California P, 1969.

Munton, Ann. "Coming to a Head, 'in a head, ahead' of Us All: Connecting with Book 5." *Tracing the Paths*. Ed. Roy Miki. Vancouver: Talonbooks, 1988. 204-230.

____. "The Long Poem as Poetic Diary." Long-liners Conference Issue. *Open Letter* 6.2-3 (1985): 93-106.

Neuman, Shirley. "'Making in a Universe of Making' in *The Martyrology*." *Tracing the Paths*. Ed. Roy Miki. Vancouver: Talonbooks, 1988. 52-70.

Nichol, bp. *ABC The Aleph Beth Book*. Ottawa: Oberon, 1971.

____. *Absolute Statement for my Mother*. Toronto: Seripress, 1979.

____. *An H in the Heart: bpNichol: A Reader*. Ed. George Bowering and Michael Ondaatje. Toronto: McClelland and Stewart Modern Canadian Poets Series, 1994.

____. "An Interview with bpNichol in Torino, May 6 & 8, 1987." With Flavio Multineddu. *Open Letter* 8.7 (1993): 5-35.

____. *art facts: a book of contexts*. Tucson, Chax P, 1990.

____. "bpNichol." Interview with Caroline Bayard and Jack David. *Out-Posts / Avant-Postes*. Three Solitudes: Contemporary Literary Criticism in Canada 4. Erin: Press Porcepic, 1978. 15-49.

____, ed. *The Cosmic Chef Glee & Perloo Memorial Society Under the Direction of Captain Poetry Presents an Evening of Concrete Courtesy Oberon Cement Works*. Ottawa: Oberon, 1970.

____. "A Contributed Editorial." *Open Letter* 3.9 (1978): 35-37.

____, ed. *Ganglia Press Index*. Toronto: Ganglia P, 1972.

____. "In Tens/tion: Dialoguing with bp." *Tracing the Paths*. Ed. Roy Miki. With Steve McCaffery. Vancouver: Talonbooks / Line, 1988. 72-91.

____. *Journeying and the Returns*. Toronto: Coach House P, 1967.

____. *The Martyrology Books 1 & 2*. Toronto: Coach House P, 1972.

____. *The Martyrology Books 3 & 4*. Toronto: Coach House P, 1976.

____. *The Martyrology Book 5*. Toronto: Coach House P, 1982.

____. *The Martyrology Book 6 Books*. Toronto: Coach House P, 1987.

____. *The Martyrology: gIFTS: Book(s) 7 &*. Toronto: Coach House P,

1990.

____. *Motherlove*. LP. Toronto: Allied Records, 1968.

____. "Passwords: The bisset papers." *Brick* 23 (1985): 5-18.

____. "The "Pata of Letter Feet, or, The English Written Character as a Medium for Poetry." *Open Letter* 6.1 (1985): 79-95.

____. "Re-discovery of the 22 letter alphabet: An Archaeological Report" *Open Letter* 4.6-7 (1980-81): 41-47.

____. *Selected Organs: Parts of an Autobiography*. Windsor: Black Moss P, 1988.

____, ed. *Steve McCaffery*. *Open Letter* 6.9 (1987).

____. *Still Water*. Vancouver: Talonbooks, 1970.

____. "'Syntax Equals the Body Structure': bpNichol, in Conversation, with Daphne Marlatt and George Bowering." Ed. Roy Miki. *Line* 6 (1985): 22-44.

____. "Talking about the Sacred in Writing." *Tracing the Paths*. Ed. Roy Miki. Vancouver: Talonbooks, 1988. 233-236.

____. "Things I don't really understand about myself." (alternate title in Table of Contents: "NOTEBOOK: a composition on composition.") *Open Letter* 6.2-3 (1985): 13, 20, 25, 39, 49. 62, 69, 73, 80, 87. 95. 102, 108, 118, 132, 141, 148, 152, 156, 228, 258, 277, 285, 292, 308, 323.

____. *Zygal: A Book of Mysteries and Translations*. Toronto: Coach House P, 1985.

Nichol, bp, and Frank Davey. "The Book as a Unit of Composition." *Open Letter* 6.1 (1985): 39-46.

____. "The Prosody of Open Verse." *The Contemporary Canadian Poem Anthology*. Ed, George Bowering. Toronto: Coach House P, 1983.

Niechoda, Irene. *A Sourcery for Books 1 and 2 of bpNichol's The Martyrology*. Toronto: ECW P, 1992.

Nietzsche, Friedrich. "On Truth and Lies in a Nonmoral Sense." 1873. *Philosophy and Truth: Selections from Nietzsche's Notebooks of the Early 1870s*. Trans. and Ed. Daniel Breazeale. Atlantic Highlands, N.J.: Humanities P, 1979. 77-97.

O'Huigan, Sean. "The Child in Him." *Open Letter* 6.5-6 (1986): 211-214.

Oliver, Kelly. *Reading Kristeva*. Bloomington: Indiana UP, 1993.

Ondaatje, Michael, ed. *The Long Poem Anthology*. Toronto: Coach House P, 1979.

Owen, D.M. "Ineluctable Seduction." Rev. of Steve McCaffery's *The Black Debt. Paragraph* 13.1 (1991): 28-29.

Perelman, Bob. "Language Writing and Literary History." *Aerial 8: Barrett Watten*. Washington: Aerial/Edge, 1995.

Perloff, Marjorie. *Radical Artifice: Writing Poetry in the Age of Media*. Chicago: U of Chicago P, 1991.

\_\_\_\_. "'Violence and Precision': The Manifesto as Art Form." *Chicago Review* 34.2 (1984): 65-101.

\_\_\_\_. "'Voice Whilst Through Thither Flood': Steve McCaffery's *Panopticon* and *North of Intention*." *Poetic Licence: Essays on Modernist and Postmodernist Lyric*. Evanston: Northwestern UP, 1990. 285-296.

Pound, Ezra. *ABC of Reading*. New York: New Directions, 1934.

Pound, Scott. "The Text Stripped Bare by Her Bachelors: A Note on Steve McCaffery's Critical Writings." Unpublished Manuscript, 1996.

Quartermain, Peter. *Disjunctive Poetics: From Gertrude Stein and Louis Zukofsky to Susan Howe*. Cambridge: Cambridge UP, 1992.

Riffaterre, Michael. *Semiotics of Poetry*. Bloomington: Indiana UP, 1978.

Rothenberg, Jerome. ed. *Shaking the Pumpkin: Traditional Poetry of the Indian North Americas*. New York: Doubleday, 1972.

Sartre, Jean Paul. *Being and Nothingness*. 1943. Trans. Hazel E. Barnes. New York: Washington Square P, 1956.

Saussure, Ferdinand de. *Course In General Linguistics*. 1916. Trans. Roy Harris. La Salle, illinois: Open Court, 1983.

Scobie, Stephen. *bpNichol: What History Teaches*. Vancouver: Talonbooks, 1984.

\_\_\_\_. "Surviving the Paraph-raise." *Read the Way he Writes: A Festschrift for bpNichol*. Ed. Paul Dutton and Steven Smith. *Open Letter* 6.5-6 (1986): 49-68.

Serafin, Bruce. "Colonial Mentalities." *Books in Canada* 19.8 (1990): 21-23.

Shattuck, Roger. "Introduction." *Selected Works of Alfred Jarry*. Ed. Roger Shattuck and Simon Watson Taylor. London: Methuen, 1965. 9-20.

Sheridan, Alan. "Translator's Note" *Ecrits: A Selection*. By Jacques Lacan. Trans. Alan Sheridan. New York: W.W. Norton & Co, 1977. vii-xii.

Silliman, Ron. *The New Sentence*. New York: Roof, 1987.

Silverman, Kaja. *The Subject of Semiotics*. New York: Oxford UP, 1983.

Solt, Mary Ellen, ed. *Concrete Poetry: A World View*. Bloomington: Indiana UP, 1968.

Steiner, George. *After Babel*. 2nd ed. New York: Oxford UP, 1992.

Sussman, Elizabeth., ed. *on the passage of a few people through a rather brief moment in time: THE SITUATIONIST INTERNATIONAL 1957-1972*. Cambridge: MIT P, 1989.

Tallman, Warren. *In The Midst*. Vancouver: Talonbooks, 1992.

Taylor, Mark C. "Non-Negative Negative Atheology." *Diacritics* 20.4 (1990): 2-16.

___. "Series Editor's Foreword." *The Book of Margins*. By Edmond Jabès. 1975. Trans. Rosemarie Waldrop. Chicago: U of Chicago P, 1993. ix-xvii.

Thesen, Sharon, ed. *The New Long Poem Anthology*. Toronto: Coach House P, 1991.

Weir, Lorraine. "Normalizing the Subject: Linda Hutcheon and the English-Canadian Postmodern." *Canadian Canons: Essays in Literary Value*. Ed. Robert Lecker. Toronto: U of Toronto P, 1991. 180-195.

Wordsworth, William. *The Prelude*. 1799, 1805, 1850. Ed. Jonathan Wordsworth, M.H. Abrams, and Stephen Gill. New York: Norton, 1979.

Wright, Elizabeth, ed. *Feminism and Psychoanalysis: A Critical Dictionary*. Oxford: Basil Blackwell, 1992.

Žižek, Slavoj. *For They Know Not What They Do: Enjoyment as a Political Factor*. London: Verso, 1991.

___. *The Sublime Object of Ideology*. London: Verso, 1989.

___. *Tarrying with the Negative*. Durham: Duke UP, 1993.

Zukofsky, Louis. *"A"*. Berkeley: U of California P, 1978.

Zukofsky, Louis, and Celia Zukofsky. *Catullus*. London: Cape Goliard, 1969.

# Index